The Startup of Seinfeld

A Multimedia Approach to Learning Entrepreneurship

By R. Scott Livengood, The Seinfeld Sensei

The Startup of Seinfeld

A Multimedia Approach to Learning Entrepreneurship

By R. Scott Livengood, The Seinfeld Sensei

ISBN: 978-1-7351756-0-7

Cover photo by Mohamed Almari
Interior graphics by Design Pickle

Table of Contents

Preface   i

Chapter 1: Entrepreneurial Process   1
Chapter 2: Becoming an Entrepreneur   7
Chapter 3: Entrepreneurial Characteristics   17
Chapter 4: Personal Entrepreneurial Risks   27
Chapter 5: Entrepreneurial Opportunities   33
Chapter 6: Entrepreneurial Product/Service Characteristics   43
Chapter 7: Entrepreneurial Assessment   53
Chapter 8: Entrepreneurial Adoption   63
Chapter 9: Entrepreneurial Business Models   73
Chapter 10: Entrepreneurial Financing   83
Chapter 11: Entrepreneurial Planning   93
Chapter 12: Entrepreneurial Pitching   105
Chapter 13: Intellectual Property Protection   117
Chapter 14: Entrepreneurial Marketing   135
Chapter 15: Founding Team   149
Chapter 16: Entrepreneurial Advice Networks   159
Chapter 17: Social Entrepreneurship   167
Chapter 18: International Entrepreneurship   173
Chapter 19: Criminal Entrepreneurship   179

References   184
Quick Episode Reference Guide   185

Preface

In the summer of 2000, I was living in Berkeley, California, doing a rotation in the Forensic and Litigation Services Practice of KPMG. Looking for something to help keep me occupied during my commute to the city and while living in a rented room with no cable, I stumbled into a used bookstore, where I came across *Seinfeld and Philosophy*. The book was written by professors of philosophy who used the context of *Seinfeld* to explore and to explain various aspects of that discipline. Although I had long been interested in the topic, I couldn't bring myself to invest time in such a complex and sophisticated subject. But the beauty of this book was that it allowed me to study topics using language and situations to which I could relate via my favorite show. Others have since explored complex philosophical principles in a wide array of popular culture contexts that are also near and dear to my heart, such as *The Simpsons, The Matrix, Star Wars, Star Trek, Harry Potter, The Lord of the Rings*, Led Zeppelin, and so on. This concept inspired me as I later pursued my PhD in strategic management and began teaching college students about the finer points of strategy and entrepreneurship—and *Seinfeld*.

Although *Seinfeld* was conceived as a "show about nothing," this book is an attempt to change that. The creators and writers were aiming for entertainment or, at most, some social commentary on the lives of a co median and his friends living on the Upper West Side of Manhattan during the 1990s. This book explores various aspects of startups and entrepreneurship, using examples from the show to illustrate those entrepreneurial principles (usually by demonstrating exactly what not to do). In this way this book becomes a critique of how the characters in *Seinfeld* are exemplars of how not to achieve entrepreneurial success, while simultaneously admitting the show was never an attempt to do otherwise.

Each chapter first presents concepts or principles about entrepreneurship grounded in theory, experience, and research, with reflection questions to help readers ponder and apply the principles to their own situations, prompted by this graphic:

Reflection Question

It then uses situations from *Seinfeld* to illustrate a practical application of these concepts, prompted by the following graphic (*sensei* means "teacher" in Japanese):

Seinfeld Sensei Application

Some liberty and creative license have been taken to make such a connection, but the intent is to educate and entertain at the same time, all the while appreciating the genius that is a show about nothing. Not that there's anything wrong with that . . . . .

Disclaimer

The *Seinfeld* clips referenced in this book are neither supported nor sponsored by the copyright holder and are included under fair use principles for educational purposes only. A list of the clips by chapter is included at the end of this book.

Although primarily an educational book, *The Startup of Seinfeld* is not meant to be a step-by-step guidebook to starting a new business or creating the next "killer app." Most of the information provided herein might be extremely valuable in helping steer readers through their entrepreneurial journeys, but the book is neither a guarantee of success nor an exhaustive exploration of the startup world and field of entrepreneurship. In addition, the author is not a lawyer, psychiatrist, or otherwise-licensed professional (rather, he is a strategic management PhD and retired CPA), so any advice gleaned from this book should be implemented in conjunction with consultation of the appropriate subject matter expert.

How to Use This Book

Each video example can be accessed in various ways. If reading an e-book on a device with an internet connection, simply clicking on the URL link will lead to the relevant clip. If reading a print version or on an e-reader/tablet without an internet connection, a QR code has been provided for access via mobile device (such as a cell phone). Readers should download a QR reader from their Apple App Store or Google Play Store to access the clip via the QR code, although some recent camera phones have a built-in QR reader that allows one to simply point the camera at the QR code and follow the link that appears. Data and streaming rates may apply.

R. Scott Livengood

Chapter 1: Entrepreneurial Process

Big Question Question: What is entrepreneurship and the entrepreneurial mindset?

Reflection Question: What does "entrepreneurship" mean to you?

Entrepreneurship Defined

What is entrepreneurship? Numerous definitions of entrepreneurship exist, and the common default is "any attempt to create a new business." This definition, however, restricts entrepreneurial activities to just new or nascent organizations. Although entrepreneurship certainly has ties to the creation of new business entities, it is much more than that particular outcome. What about incumbent companies that already exist? Are they not able to be entrepreneurial? And what about new businesses that simply imitate or replicate what others are doing and don't differentiate in any meaningful way? Would they be considered entrepreneurial?

In this book, the focus is on the **entrepreneurial mindset**, which can be applied to all kinds of situations and by all kinds of people. At its essence, the entrepreneurial mindset is about the art and craft of the creative, the unexpected, and the exceptional. This mindset focuses on creating something new and valuable by providing solutions that are better, faster, and/or cheaper than others. This mindset highlights continuous improvement and not being complacent. A critical aspect of the entrepreneurial mindset is learning from and managing mistakes.

A working definition of entrepreneurship might be "opportunity recognition and action under conditions of extreme uncertainty and limited resources." **Opportunity** is defined as market failure or imperfect market conditions, instances in which customers want something but can't get it—they have a problem, but no effective solution exists, or a better solution is possible. Therefore, entrepreneurial action is needed to creatively solve those problems in a manner that customers will adopt and for which they are willing to pay. Entrepreneurs must manage and reduce the risk-reward equation (for customers and for themselves) and must then *act* with the tenacity to push an idea through to reality.

Entrepreneurial Process

The entrepreneurial process thus becomes a cycle of **identifying opportunities** or market failures (otherwise known as problems that need to be solved), using one's skills, experience, and ingenuity for **generating creative solutions** based on those opportunities, **assessing and quantifying the risk** of those solutions (ideally minimizing that risk as much as possible), **assembling resources** (but expending as few as possible) to make the solution viable, and then **presenting that solution** to interested stakeholders, which can sometimes (but not always) culminate in the formation of a new business entity or unit.

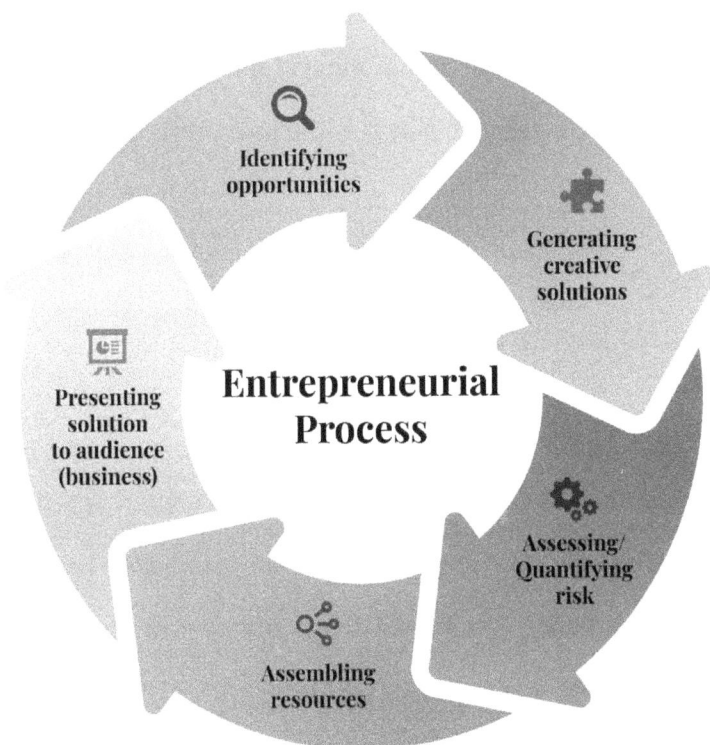

This process is rarely linear, and entrepreneurs are often required to explore numerous opportunities, validate multiple potential solutions, minimize extremely risky and uncertain situations, overcome increased resource barriers, and convince various audiences before a truly viable entrepreneurial endeavor can be deemed successful. Entrepreneurs almost never get this correct on the first try, but those who are able to persevere and to overcome these challenges not only solve real problems for others but often find great personal satisfaction, which is typically higher for entrepreneurship than for most other professional endeavors.

Reflection Question: Which part of the entrepreneurial process do you think is the most challenging? Which is the most intriguing?

Seinfeld Sensei Application

Problems often exist in people's everyday lives that are just waiting for a new and creative solution. George and Kramer recognized just such an issue with George's father, Frank, and demonstrated how the entrepreneurial process could be followed to pursue an idea.

Season 6, Episode 17 "The Doorman" (4:08)

Kramer's identification of a potentially profitable entrepreneurial opportunity began with him recognizing a problem faced by an acquaintance. He then generated a possible solution by simply reapplying one that already existed to help with a problem commonly encountered by women, which opened up a potentially new set of customers. He asked questions of his target customer centered on the pains the customer was experiencing to learn more about the underlying problem. To further reduce the potential risk of his solution not being accepted by the market, he created a prototype to test out his idea with his target customer. Part of his resource assembly process included reaching out to potential partners to help with the manufacturing, branding, and distribution processes, and the positive feedback when presenting to an executive in the business helped demonstrate the immense promise of the entrepreneurial idea. Although not an ultimately successful idea, Kramer's solution exemplified how the entrepreneurial process can be followed to help solve some of society's "big" problems. This entrepreneurial process is explored in more detail throughout this book, with varying levels of success in the endeavors demonstrated by our *Seinfeld* case subjects.

Chapter 2:
Becoming an
Entrepreneur

Big Question Question: Who becomes an entrepreneur? And why?

Successful Model of Entrepreneurship

The figure below shows what I have termed the "Successful Model of Entrepreneurship," adapted from Stephen R Covey's *8th Habit: From Effectiveness to Greatness*. This model begins with the talent of the entrepreneur, which highlights what the entrepreneur is **able** to do. A great deal of experience, expertise, and various other characteristics are needed to engage in entrepreneurial activity, and this often guides entrepreneurs to pursue the types of activities for which they are most suited. Although entrepreneurs could always learn about areas for which they have no talent and experience, those who have a background in a particular area of interest tend to be better positioned to recognize problems to be solved and creative ways to solve them.

After talent comes passion, or what the entrepreneur truly **wants** to do. Passion is often necessary to keep the entrepreneur engaged and willing to sacrifice what is necessary to make an entrepreneurial endeavor successful. Passion and interest can also help increase the attention paid to issues related to the entrepreneurial idea, as people tend to notice what's happening around topics important to them. Usually talent and passion combine to form our hobbies and interests, but this rarely becomes the foundation for an occupation without the next element of the model.

Next comes **need**, which encapsulates market demand for the particular solution the entrepreneur is intending to provide. Without need, no matter what solution the entrepreneur comes up with or how brilliant it is, the entrepreneurial endeavor is likely to fail. Sometimes "need" can be replaced by what the market "wants," as not all successful products or services can be appropriately classified as a "need." Either way market demand is necessary to ensure the entrepreneurial idea becomes a successful business endeavor.

Finally, the model suggests the importance of conscience, or whether or not the entrepreneur **should** engage in such activity at all. Although the idea of ethics, and even legality, can be a matter of perception, entrepreneurial activity that may be questionable from an ethical or legal perspective (such as price gouging during a crisis or misrepresenting a product's or service's capabilities) is not sustainable. The weight on one's mind and heart of engaging in activities one shouldn't be can interfere with long-term health and happiness.

"Successful" Model of Entrepreneurship

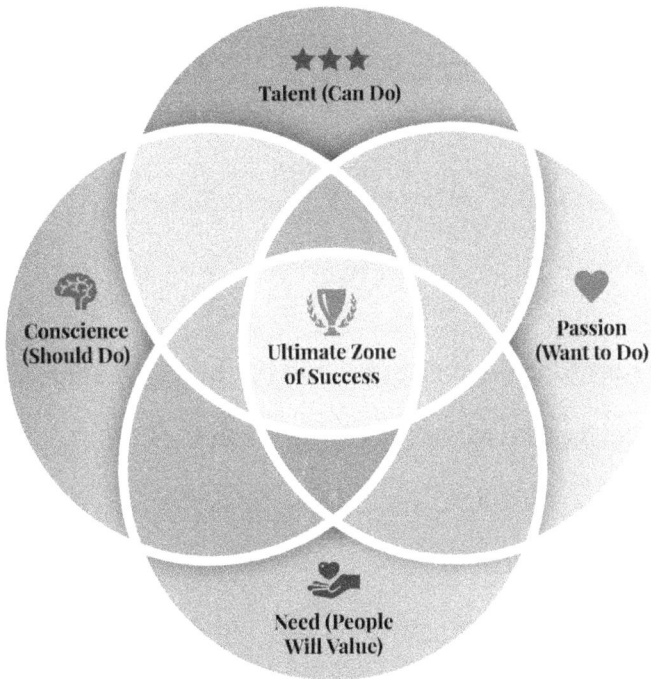

★★★
Talent (Can Do)

**Conscience
(Should Do)**

**Ultimate Zone
of Success**

**Passion
(Want to Do)**

**Need (People
Will Value)**

Reflection Question: How do you define success?

At the intersection of all of these elements is what I call the "Ultimate Zone of Success." In this context success is not limited merely to financial performance but also overall happiness and satisfaction within all areas of life. When all of these areas are aligned, the likelihood of success and happiness is greatly increased. This is similar to the Japanese concept of *ikigai* (reason for being) but with more of an emphasis on entrepreneurial activity. For example, *ikigai* separates what people need and what people will pay for into one circle, excluding the conscience aspect of the Successful Model of Entrepreneurship.

Reflection Question: What elements of your life do you think exist at the center of the Successful Model of Entrepreneurship?

Becoming an Entrepreneur

All kinds of people become entrepreneurs, and they do so for various reasons. Although those reasons are usually personal, the following list includes the most common reasons for people to become entrepreneurs.

1. **The need for independence/autonomy/flexibility.** Some people don't like working for someone else and would rather be their own boss, with more opportunity to do things their own way. Unfortunately even entrepreneurs have bosses . . . usually called "the customer."

2. **The desire for personal development/challenge:** Often people are looking for an opportunity to test themselves and to enjoy the feeling of satisfaction that comes from solving a real problem. Entrepreneurship provides people with an opportunity to solve issues faced by themselves and by others.

3. **Pursue an idea/passion:** Some entrepreneurs are inspired by solving a problem that is important to them or to others they care about and are therefore passionate about finding a solution.

4. **Welfare (philanthropic) considerations:** Particularly in the realm of social entrepreneurship, the purpose for pursuing an entrepreneurial idea extends beyond profits and aims to help the environment, underprivileged groups, or other social causes.

5. **Leave a legacy:** Creating a successful entrepreneurial firm sometimes leads to a business that lasts decades, and the impact of that business can be felt long after the founder is no longer involved.

6. **Follow role models:** Some people have seen or experienced how family members or others in their local community have improved their lives or the lives of those around them through entrepreneurial endeavors and want to follow in those footsteps.

7. **Financial independence:** Although the risks of entrepreneurial activities tend to be high, the monetary rewards can also be enormous, allowing entrepreneurs to achieve their financial goals.

Common Reasons For
People to Become Entrepreneurs

1 The need for independence/ autonomy/flexibility (no boss)	**2** The desire for personal development/ challenge
3 Pursue an idea/passion	**4** Welfare (philanthropic) considerations
5 Leave a legacy	**6** Follow role models
7 Financial independence	

Why is this important? Why might one care about the reasons for being an entrepreneur? One reason might be motivation: Entrepreneurial pursuits often require sacrifice, with many long and lonely days and nights involving hardship, rejection, and disappointment, so a periodic reminder of why entrepreneurs got into this to begin with can act as a motivator to help in overcoming those obstacles.

Reflection Question: Why might you want to be an entrepreneur? Are there other reasons not listed above that interest you?

Sometimes people become entrepreneurs reluctantly. Such entrepreneurs usually have stable jobs but are interested in starting something on their own, so they slowly start an endeavor on the side. Once these secondary pursuits grow and become so successful that they take over their day jobs, they leave to go pursue their entrepreneurial ideas. Even this, however, is a quite risky endeavor, so it often takes a particular type of person to abandon the safety of an established career and steady paycheck for the possibility of entrepreneurial success, as I discuss below.

Others work for a company that is either unwilling or unable to pursue certain niches in the market wherein the individual sees an opportunity. Sometimes those employees leave the existing firm to create spinoffs, allowing them to put their ideas into practice. These entrepreneurs can leverage their industry experience and expertise to capitalize on opportunities in the marketplace.

Seinfeld Sensei Application

George was frustrated with his boss, and his desire for autonomy and independence caused him to pursue other options.

Season 2, Episode 7 "The Revenge" (3:33)

George did a fantastic job with the first two sections of the Successful Model of Entrepreneurship by initially identifying areas in which he had some talent and passion. Jerry, as a loyal and helpful friend, aided George in identifying obstacles that might inhibit him from pursuing these talents and passions as occupations, since the market might not value George's potential contributions. So even though George had many things he was interested in doing, these may not have aligned with what he could do and was qualified to do, nor with what others might have valued.

Chapter 3: Entrepreneurial Characteristics

Big Question Question: What are characteristics common to those with an entrepreneurial mindset?

Scholars of entrepreneurship have tried to identify lists of characteristics that encapsulate the entrepreneurial mindset. Some of these are included on the following page.

Reflection Question: Which of the following characteristics are unique to entrepreneurs as opposed to those applicable to anyone wanting to be successful? For example, almost anything one wants to do requires determination and perseverance, but which of these characteristics are especially important for the entrepreneurial mindset as differentiated from other pursuits?

Entrepreneurial Characteristics

- Determination and perseverance
- Ability to learn from mistakes
- Drive to achieve
- Flexibility
- Opportunity orientation
- Initiative and responsibility
- Persistent problem solving
- Seeking feedback
- Internal locus of control
- Tolerance for ambiguity

- Calculated risk taking
- High energy level
- Creativity and innovativeness
- Vision
- Passion
- Independence
- Resourcefulness
- Team building
- Optimism
- Confidence

One key insight to keep in mind is that no *one* right way to be an entrepreneur exists, so individuals involved in entrepreneurial activities can be successful even though they might not possess all the above characteristics. Certainly some of the above-mentioned characteristics can be useful, but simply having those characteristics is often not enough, and not having those characteristics doesn't mean one can't be successful. The importance thus lies in each entrepreneur recognizing what is needed to be successful, identifying strengths and weaknesses, and making the necessary adjustments.

Overcoming Lack of Desirable Characteristics

Entrepreneurs who have identified areas in which they are lacking should work to develop the necessary characteristics or hire/partner with someone who possesses those characteristics to help compensate for what the entrepreneur lacks. Rarely does one person possess all the skills, abilities, and characteristics necessary to build, grow, and sustain a profitable enterprise.

For example, if entrepreneurs are lacking in public speaking skills, they can take classes, join clubs, or simply practice presenting in public. They might alternatively hire someone else to complete any public speaking requirements for the firm, which would allow entrepreneurs to focus on their strengths and at the same time encourage others to contribute their strengths toward the overall benefit of the firm.

Reflection Question: What are some strengths you possess that would be beneficial to a startup team? What weaknesses do you possess that you would want to overcome, and how would you do so?

Seinfeld Sensei Application

Kramer attempted a change to his lifestyle to try to develop creativity and to free up more time for his entrepreneurial pursuits. He decided to borrow from the life of Leonardo da Vinci by adopting a particular sleeping practice that helped the Master with his innovative activities.

Season 7, Episode 18 "The Friar's Club" (4:52)

Unfortunately, Kramer provided a good example of how trying to be someone one's not might lead to rather undesirable consequences—namely, waking up in the Hudson River in a sack! Aspiring entrepreneurs should take stock of their strengths and weaknesses and strive to become better for their pursuits, but ultimately being oneself is the best kind of entrepreneur one can be.

In another example, George demonstrated the difficulties that exist in overcoming certain weaknesses, illustrating how important some of those skills are to being successful.

Season 6, Episode 17 "The Jimmy" (3:40)

Here George was unable to convince others of the benefits of his product, yet Jimmy's ability to jump could have done just that. Entrepreneurs often need to hire or partner with others to help compensate for their weaknesses.

Regarding the concept of partnering with others to compensate for a lack of a needed characteristic or ability, the *Seinfeld* gang demonstrated how recognizing rare skills in others can be useful.

Season 5, Episode 6 "The Lip Reader" (4:07)

The beautiful lineswoman Laura possessed a unique skill for reading lips, which George wanted to leverage to learn what his ex-girlfriend said about him. Although the actual application of this skill didn't work for George, creating a team or hiring employees with skills the entrepreneur doesn't possess can be an effective way to capitalize on opportunities and to overcome a lack of skills or expertise in important areas.

Entrepreneurial Ego

Although most entrepreneurs are examined in a positive light, not all are role models or exemplify positive characteristics. The "Entrepreneurial Ego" is well documented, and often creative, visionary entrepreneurs are very difficult to work with and for. Some of the characteristics relevant to this type include:

Entrepreneurial Ego

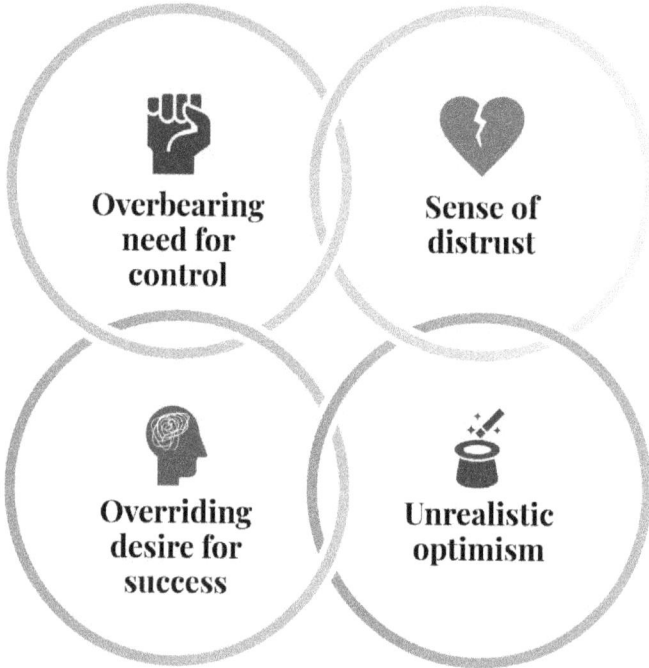

- **Overbearing need for control.** Some entrepreneurs are perfectionists, which often leads to micromanaging employees to make sure work is done in accordance with their unrealistically high expectations.
- **Sense of distrust.** This can lead to paranoia where entrepreneurs can think employees are going to steal their ideas or are not committed to working hard enough for the entrepreneurial endeavor to succeed.

- **Overriding desire for success.** Although perseverance is a desirable quality, some entrepreneurs are so focused on achieving their goals that they can't admit defeat or failure, even when all signs indicate a change is needed.
- **Unrealistic optimism.** Healthy amounts of self-efficacy and confidence are often necessary to be successful, but too much can impede entrepreneurs' ability to accept criticism or mentoring to ensure goals are reasonable and attainable.

Seinfeld Sensei Application

An acquaintance of Kramer's can help shed some light on why entrepreneurs sometimes exhibit the negative characteristics of the entrepreneurial ego.

Season 7, Episode 6 "The Soup Nazi" (1:59)

Kramer explained why the so-called "Soup Nazi" acted the way he did: He had extremely high expectations of himself, which helped push him to be creative and successful, so why shouldn't he expect the same level of dedication and professionalism from his customers? The Soup Nazi certainly was overbearing in his need for control, didn't seem to trust his customers to act appropriately, and let his overwhelming pursuit of perfection interfere with a focus on customer service. So although this kind of behavior may not be excused, hopefully it can at least be somewhat understood as a manifestation of the entrepreneurial ego.

In another example Jerry encountered a mechanic who demonstrated a high degree of passion for his craft, which caused him to also have high expectations from his customers.

Season 7, Episode 20 "The Bottle Deposit" (3:56)

Tony the mechanic was rather overbearing and took matters into his own hands to try to take care of Jerry's car. Although his dedication is certainly to be commended, it also caused him to take situations to the extreme, leaving collateral damage in his wake.

Chapter 4:
Personal
Entrepreneurial Risks

Big Question Question: What personal risks do entrepreneurs face?

Although many positive outcomes can come from entrepreneurial pursuits, entrepreneurship can have a downside as well—namely, the high degree of risk involved with such endeavors. The terms "risk" and "uncertainty" are often used interchangeably, but they actually apply to quite different contexts. **Risk** is usually used to quantify a level of likelihood of a desired outcome, where the risk of failure is, for example, 80 percent. This opens up the subjective nature of how to view that outcome, where some people might consider an 80 percent failure rate to be too risky, while others might be willing to take that risk. **Uncertainty**, on the other hand, is used when quantifying the likelihood of an outcome can't even be reliably calculated. The conditions, terms, and unknowns are such that quantification is difficult or impossible. Risk tends to be a result of uncertainty, as a higher number of unknowns make outcomes harder to predict or control and therefore increase potential errors of quantification.

The world of entrepreneurship by its very nature deals with a great deal of uncertainty, primarily because entrepreneurs are innovative, creative, and are doing things that haven't been done the same way before. Because of this newness, past experience or current benchmarks become unreliable, increasing the difficulty of quantifying risk in any meaningful way. Thus, being able to predict the market demand, technological difficulty, financial return, competitive response, organizational challenges, and so forth for a startup becomes exceptionally difficult to do. This type of risk and uncertainty will be covered in subsequent chapters, but alongside those factors is the personal risk faced by those who want to become entrepreneurs.

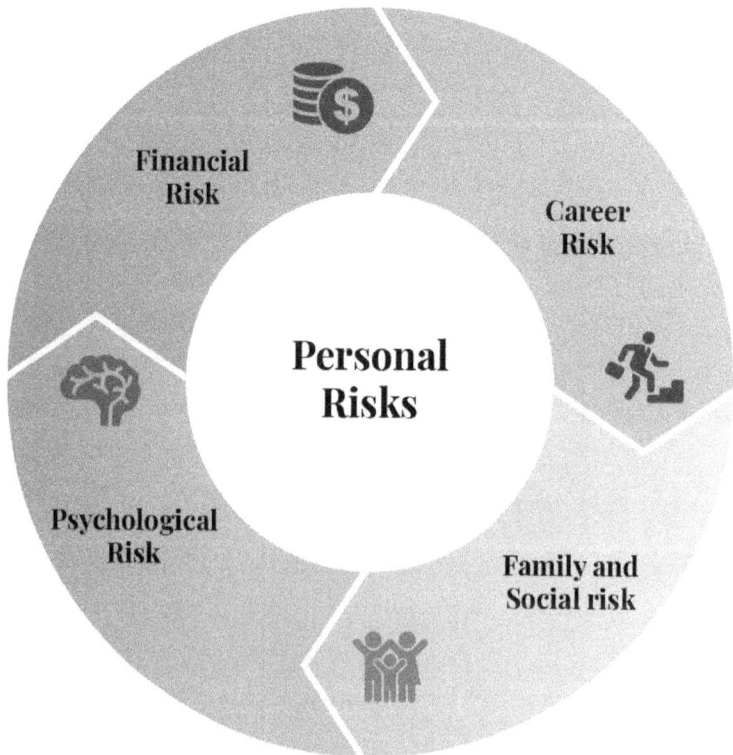

Entrepreneurs face **financial risk** where they don't have a steady or even predictable income and have to work diligently to obtain their next paycheck, sacrificing a steady salary for the promise of a successful enterprise. In addition, **career risk** involves an increase in the loss of employment security, which heightens the importance of the new venture's success. Further, **family and social risk** involves competing commitments between work and family that often make it difficult for entrepreneurs to balance between these interests. Finally, because of the high likelihood of setbacks along the way, entrepreneurs must be able to handle the **psychological risk** of their startup failing, which can impact self-esteem and job satisfaction.

Reflection Question: Among the personal risks of entrepreneurship, which are of most concern to you? What might you do to reduce this risk?

Seinfeld Sensei Application

Although not necessarily housed in an entrepreneurial context, Kramer and Jerry showed how the pressures of work could impact a usually harmonious relationship.

Season 8, Episode 3 "The Bizarro Jerry" (4:31)

Kramer and Jerry's attempt to adjust to the strains and stresses of a new job demonstrated the family and social risk that can come from entrepreneurial and business pursuits. Rather than enjoying the freedom entrepreneurship can bring, Kramer sought the structure of a corporate job. However, as can happen in all business endeavors, the pressures of working strained the domestic relationship between Jerry and Kramer, even though Kramer didn't technically even work at that office!

Entrepreneurs have to deal with a lot of risk and uncertainty, and some have a greater psychological ability to handle the ups and downs that come from the financial performance of a venture than others. George and Jerry seemed to have different risk profiles when dealing with a certain stock tip.

Season 1, Episode 5 "The Stock Tip" (3:42)

Jerry struggled with the risk involved in the stock market, an entity whose volatility is very similar to that of many entrepreneurial ventures. George also struggled at first, but his willingness to stick with the stock paid off in the end. Entrepreneurs who aren't able to deal with the psychological and emotional risk of their endeavors might struggle when faced with extreme uncertainty and the unpredictability of financial success.

Chapter 5:
Entrepreneurial
Opportunities

Big Question Question: What are the sources of good ideas?

Opportunity Identification

The genesis of entrepreneurial action begins with identifying an opportunity or an important problem to be solved, which then leads to new ideas to solve the problem contained in the opportunity. Opportunity identification is central to entrepreneurship, as the latter involves the creative pursuit of ideas and an innovative process for coming up with "good ideas." Although this process is rarely easy, successful opportunity recognition, creative problem solving, and effective execution can lead to both personal and societal successes and mutually beneficial outcomes. The role of the entrepreneur is to analyze the situation, to seek out/create innovative solutions to fill customer needs and wants, and to turn problems into opportunities.

User Entrepreneurs

Sometimes these good ideas come from what are called "user entrepreneurs." These are people who are using a product or service or engaging in an activity that is not fully satisfying their own needs. They are essentially already customers and are able to identify problems and creative solutions based on their own personal experiences. One person's own experience, however, may not be the same as those of others, and just because a (potentially idiosyncratic) solution solves the entrepreneur's own problem doesn't mean it will become a successful entrepreneurial endeavor.

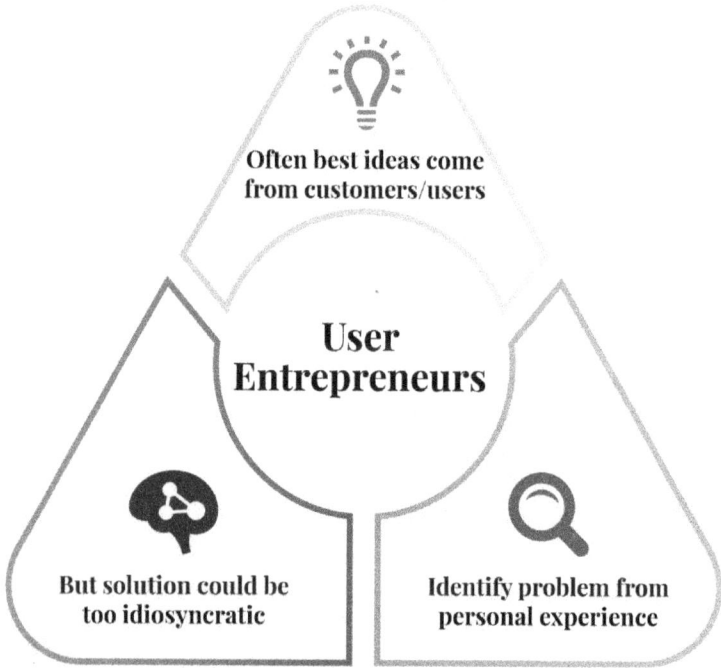

Often best ideas come from customers/users

User Entrepreneurs

But solution could be too idiosyncratic

Identify problem from personal experience

Reflection Question: What is an example from your own life of an ineffective solution to a problem you have faced?

Seinfeld Sensei Application

An important part of the entrepreneurial mindset is seeing the world in a different way. Often entrepreneurs have unique insights based on their lives and vocational experiences that cause them to see things in ways others don't. George embarked on a journey of experimentation with creative and innovative ways to govern his life—a journey that is often a source of entrepreneurial opportunities.

Season 5, Episode 22 "The Opposite" (4:44)

For those who don't see themselves as particularly creative or entrepreneurial, perhaps doing something different, something weird, or something new can be a way to get in touch with the little entrepreneur inside each of us. George's new philosophy and outlook for life benefited him in unexpected ways, and if entrepreneurs are looking for new perspectives and solutions to existing problems, perhaps a change of routine could be the stimulus needed for increased creativity and entrepreneurial vision.

Identifying Trends

Innovative ideas can have several different sources. Some of them include:

- **Black Swan** events are low-likelihood, high-impact events very few people could have expected, such as a contagious virus. For those who are able to recognize how things have changed and to identify new needs and wants in the altered environment, entrepreneurial opportunities abound.

- **Mismatch** occurs when customer expectations are not being met, and they want something for which no current or satisfactory solution exists. By fixing this mismatch, entrepreneurs can help solve immediate problems faced by the market.

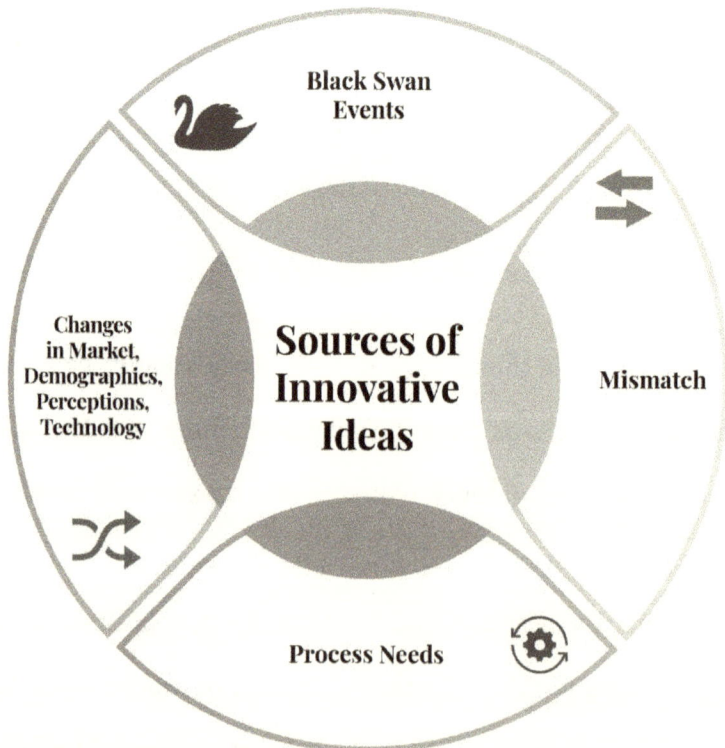

Black Swan Events

Changes in Market, Demographics, Perceptions, Technology

Sources of Innovative Ideas

Mismatch

Process Needs

- **Process needs** are situations where customers are doing something one way but want to improve how things are being done. A famous example is told of a 3M employee who was singing in his church choir and needed to switch between songs in his hymnbook. Using a piece of paper was insufficient because the paper would fall out, and paperclips damaged the pages. So he sought a temporary, low-grade adhesive from his company's research and development department, which is how Post-It Notes were created.

- **Changes** in industry/market conditions (competitor actions, customer preferences, and the general evolution in the marketplace); demographics (including age, gender, income, nationalities); perceptions (such as an increased demand for healthy, environmentally friendly, or made in home country products and services); and/or technologies/science/capabilities (some of which may occur in other industries) can all be great sources for innovative ideas and entrepreneurial inspiration.

Put another way, alert entrepreneurs need to recognize **trends** in the marketplace and either anticipate where these trends are heading or influence those trends in favor of their creative solution.

These trends can be classified using the popular PESTEL model as follows:

- Political/governmental trends (increased regulations, natural resource prices, terrorism)

- Economic trends (higher disposable incomes, dual wage-earner families)

- Societal trends (aging demographics, health and fitness growth, senior living)

- Technology trends (mobile technology, ecommerce, internet advances)

- Environmental trends (climate change, seasonality)

- Legal trends (laws and regulations, property rights, enforcement, precedent)

Identifying Trends – PESTEL

Political/Governmental   Economic   Sociocultural

Technological   Environmental   Legal

Two potentially important missing elements from the popular PESTEL framework are:

- International trends (innovations and practices in other countries)
- Competitive trends (innovations from rivals in the same industry, innovations in other industries, market adoption)

Reflection Question: What is a trend you are aware of that could be a source of entrepreneurial opportunities?

Innovation has multiple sources, but the key to coming up with good ideas is paying attention to problems and changes in one's own life and the general external environment as foundations of entrepreneurial pursuits.

Seinfeld Sensei Application

Elaine's boss, Mr. Pitt, had a unique mannerism that seemed bizarre at first but quickly caught on with the public at large.

Season 6, Episode 3 "The Pledge Drive" (3:29)

Elaine was somewhat resistant to the idea of change, but entrepreneurs usually embrace new things. Although difficulty often exists when predicting what trends or innovations might actually catch on, an alert entrepreneur is able to recognize trends gaining in popularity and turn them into good business ideas. Whether it is creating and selling disposable, environmentally-friendly spoons alongside M&M'S or similar knives and forks next to SNICKERS, entrepreneurial opportunities are all around us!

Chapter 6: Entrepreneurial Product/Service Characteristics

Big Question Question: How do entrepreneurial products and services improve the lives of customers?

Characteristics of Entrepreneurial Products and Services

Market problems or opportunities (the reason for needing entrepreneurial innovation) usually exist in one of three areas: product or service features are not satisfactory, purchasing or using the product or service is inconvenient, and/or the price of the product or service is too high relative to the value obtained. As such, entrepreneurial solutions tend to focus on making products or services **better** (new or unique features or functionalities), **faster** (or otherwise more convenient), and/or **cheaper** (lower price for consumers). Entrepreneurs must come up with new and innovative ways to satisfy customers' needs and to create value differently than what is currently offered by rivals in the marketplace.

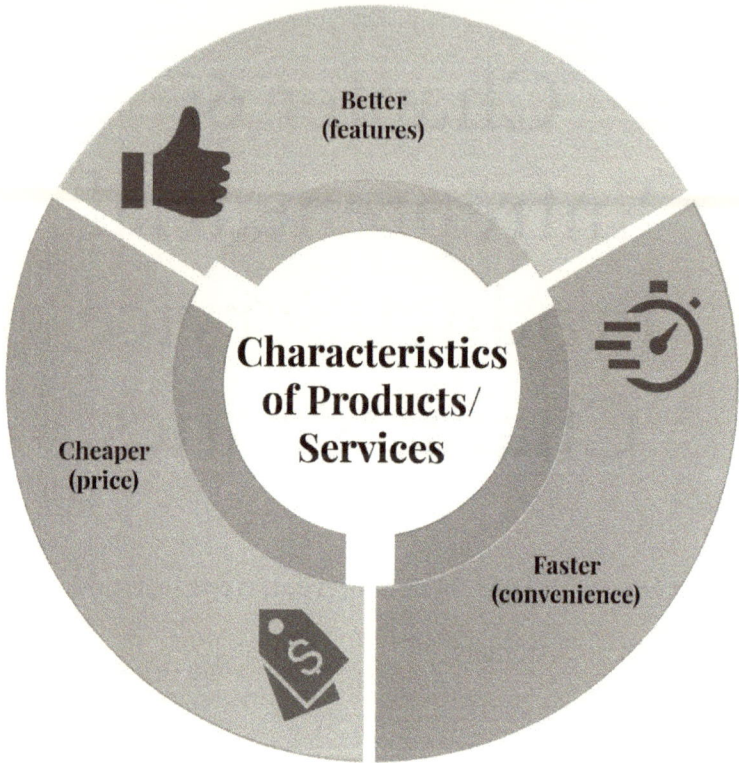

Characteristics of Products/Services

- Better (features)
- Cheaper (price)
- Faster (convenience)

Reflection Question: Is it easiest to make products and/or services *better, faster,* or *cheaper*? Why?

Seinfeld Sensei Application

A key to creating a valuable entrepreneurial product is demonstrating how much a customer's life can be improved over the status quo through the proposed product or solution. If the solution is not better, faster, and/or cheaper than what is currently being offered, the customers will most likely solve the problem themselves, which is exactly what Kramer attempted to do when looking for a place to store his blood.

Season 9, Episode 4 "The Blood" (3:58)

Kramer was fed up with the fees charged by his blood bank, so he came up with his own, cheaper alternative. In this case, keeping his blood at home also had some positive outcomes the blood bank could not provide: His blood helped save Jerry's life, which in turn earned "favors" from Jerry for both Kramer and Newman. Kramer's solution eventually caused additional problems, but the general idea is that if an entrepreneur's solution does not add value above and beyond the status quo, customers will make do or will create their own solutions.

Value Proposition

A **value proposition** communicates how an entrepreneurial idea will solve a problem or opportunity for the customer and should clearly show *how* this solution is more attractive than other options. The more demonstrable value a solution offers, the more likely it will be purchased, increasing the likelihood of success for the entrepreneurial venture. This can be done by highlighting how a customer's happiness can be increased by using the product or service, showcasing how a customer's pain could be reduced by using the product or service, or a combination of both. Research suggests value propositions demonstrating reduced pain tend to be more effective, as customers value eliminating pain over increasing pleasure. In addition, rather than just explaining the functions and features of the product or service, an effective value proposition instead focuses on the benefits received or the pain reduced for the customer. A key to creating a compelling value proposition is demonstrating how much better, faster, and/or cheaper the proposed product or solution is versus the status quo.

Value Proposition

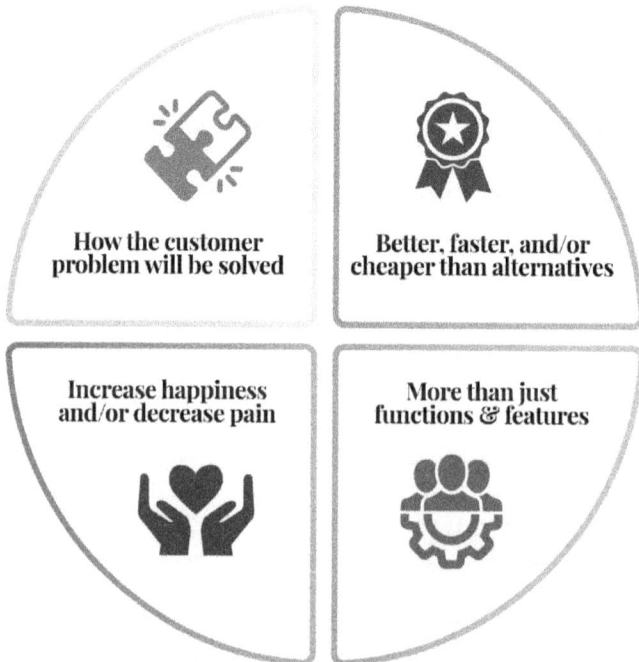

How the customer problem will be solved

Better, faster, and/or cheaper than alternatives

Increase happiness and/or decrease pain

More than just functions & features

Reflection Question: Think of a product or service you use on a regular basis. What value proposition for that product or service would resonate with you?

Seinfeld Sensei Application

One example of a value proposition centers on Jerry's introduction to an innovative pen by his parents' neighbor in Florida.

Season 3, Episode 5 "The Pen" (2:41)

The amazing characteristics of the astronaut pen that writes upside down appealed to Jerry. In classic *Seinfeld* style, his admiration had many unforeseen consequences, but in essence the innovative features of the pen, which satisfied his needs, captivated Elaine, and caused Jack to regularly brag about the pen, indicated a product that had an impactful value proposition. The fact the pen caused such a controversy in the retirement community meant the entrepreneurial characteristics of the pen were highly sought after and were certainly better than other pen offerings.

Innovation Spectrum

When creating a value proposition, understanding how the product or service compares to existing offerings is important so entrepreneurs can highlight how and why their solution is better, faster, and/or cheaper than those of their competitors. The following figure shows a spectrum of newness of ideas, which increases from left to right. As the novelty or newness increases, so too does the uncertainty related to the idea. One major source of this uncertainty stems from the fact that the idea is harder to compare to what is already in existence, which has implications for market research, planning, resource gathering, and so forth. Importantly, this uncertainty also exists for potential customers and their acceptance of the new product or service.

- **Replication** is simply copying what is being done elsewhere and starting it in a new area, with franchising or international expansion serving as examples.
- **Imitation** is copying what is being done elsewhere but making a minor adjustment or incremental improvement.
- **Modification** means making a major improvement.
- **Recombination** is taking two existing products or services and combining them in unique ways to add value or to solve a particu-

lar problem (such as adding a camera to a mobile phone).

- **Radical Innovation** is a major leap in what's currently being done that is truly unexpected and new.

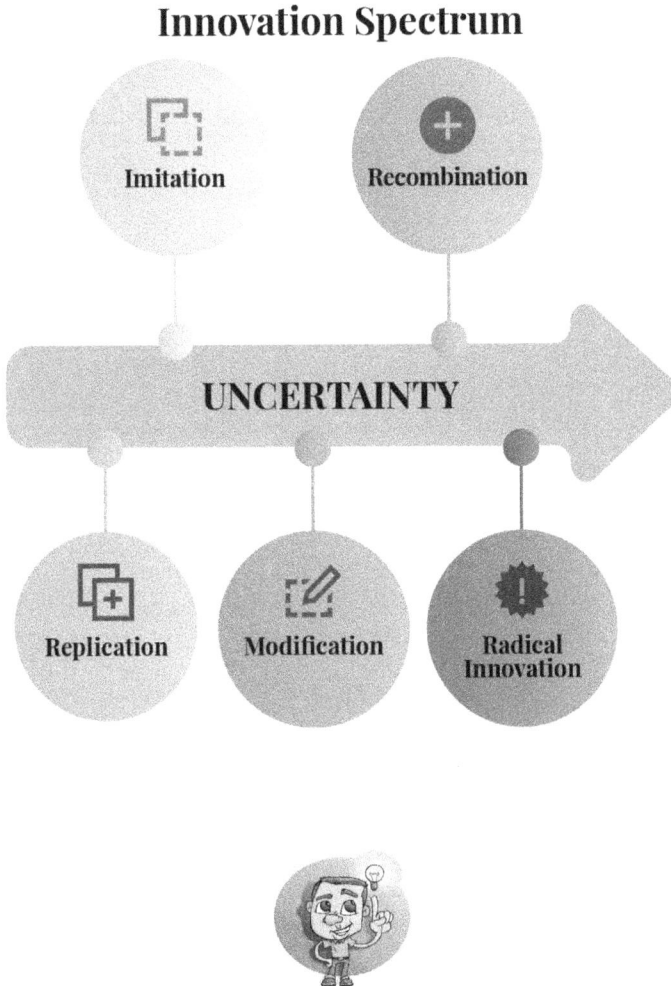

Innovation Spectrum

Imitation

Recombination

UNCERTAINTY

Replication

Modification

Radical Innovation

Reflection Question: Are any entrepreneurial ideas truly "created," meaning they are not at all derived from some other, already existing solutions? Or are most ideas simply reapplications or reconfigurations of other ideas?

Seinfeld Sensei Application

Always looking to do things his own way, George was presented with a situation that appealed to multiple passions and interests in his life.

Season 9, Episode 4 "The Blood" (3:53)

As a nice example of recombination, George explored an opportunity to combine two of his passions—food and sex—to create a more satisfactory experience. But adding TV to the equation was too much, until he found the right woman who valued his recombination of pleasurable activities. Too often, entrepreneurs create solutions and then look for problems those solutions might solve, which is usually inefficient and wasteful of valuable resources, but in this case George was fortunate to find a woman whose interests matched his own.

Chapter 7: Entrepreneurial Assessment

Big Question Question: How does one evaluate good ideas so they become good *business* ideas?

A major premise for this topic is that not all great ideas become great businesses. This could occur for several reasons (other than an idea simply being dumb):

- Market/demand might not exist
- Business model may not be feasible
- Skills/abilities of the entrepreneur or entrepreneurial team might not match the idea
- Idea is not better/faster/cheaper than alternatives

This chapter highlights ways entrepreneurs can assess whether their initial ideas have the potential to become profitable business ideas.

Startup Loop of Despair

As discussed in the *All-in Startup* book by Diana Kander, traditional approaches to entrepreneurship follow the following sequence: idea →

build → brand → customer. More specifically, ideas are generated to solve a particular problem, a product is built around that idea, it is branded and marketed, and then customers decide whether this solves their particular problem by purchasing the product (or not). But what if the customer doesn't like or is not willing to pay for this solution? The entrepreneur must take this feedback into consideration to come up with a new solution, build that solution, brand it, and then present it to the customer to determine its success. This process requires a great deal of resources in the form of time, effort, energy, and money, most of which are severely limited for entrepreneurial firms—resulting in the "Startup Loop of Despair."

Startup Loop of Despair

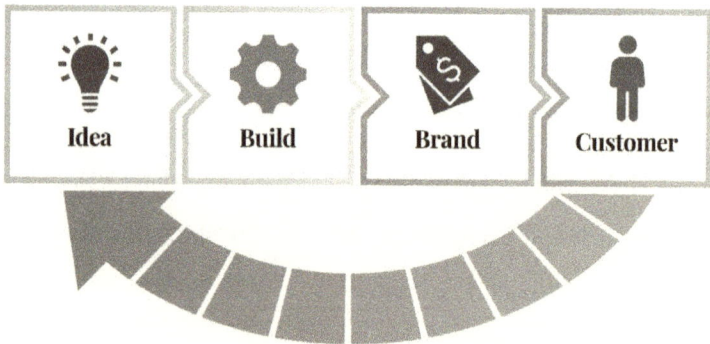

| Idea | Build | Brand | Customer |

A recent trend in entrepreneurship changes the sequence of events from this traditional model and involves the customer much earlier in the process. The **Lean Entrepreneurship** approach follows the following sequence: idea → customer → build → brand; it is designed to expend dramatically fewer resources to arrive at the appropriate customer solution. Customer feedback thus becomes extremely important to making sure the entrepreneur is on the right track before wasting valuable resources going in the wrong direction and making a product or service the customer doesn't want. One of the biggest risks of entrepreneurship is creating a product or service that nobody wants to buy.

Lean Entrepreneurship

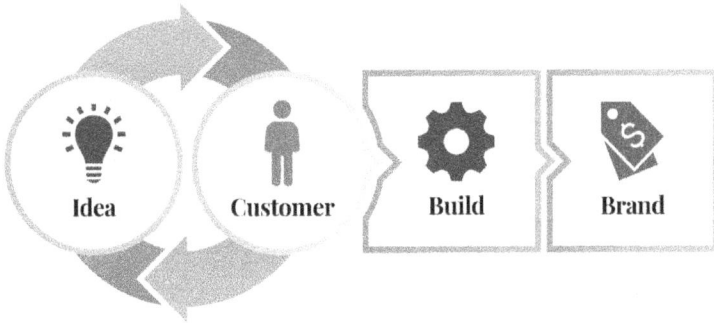

Reflection Question: As a resource-constrained entrepreneur, how many times do you think you can go through the "traditional" sequence of idea, build, brand, and customer? What potential advantages does the Lean Entrepreneurship Model provide?

Lean Entrepreneurship Model

The Lean Entrepreneurship Model starts with developing a **vision** of a potential solution and how the entrepreneur's business can help solve an important problem for the customer. Next, the entrepreneur turns that vision into testable **hypotheses**, which are best guesses about or expectations for how the idea will work and how the activities of the entrepreneur will turn the concept into reality. One central principle of lean entrepreneurship is treating everything like a hypothesis, which helps make sure the entrepreneur gets in the habit of testing out and validating new ideas before expending valuable resources chasing dead ends. This testing and validating begins with a **minimum viable product (MVP)**, a very simple prototype with basic functionality that the entrepreneur can test with potential customers to determine which functions they will find most valuable. The key is to spend the least amount of resources possible until a positive and consistent path is validated by potential customers. As the feedback is analyzed, the entrepreneur must decide whether to **persevere** (continue with the idea or original path), **pivot** (change direction of the entrepreneurial idea), or **perish** (realize the chances for the idea to succeed are extremely low). Once enough positive feedback is received for a solution, the entrepreneur should **scale** the idea to sell to more customers and **optimize** business operations around that one solution. By following this model, entrepreneurs can help ensure they are truly creating something to solve a real customer need and are discovering that by expending the least amount of resources possible.

Lean Entrepreneurship Model

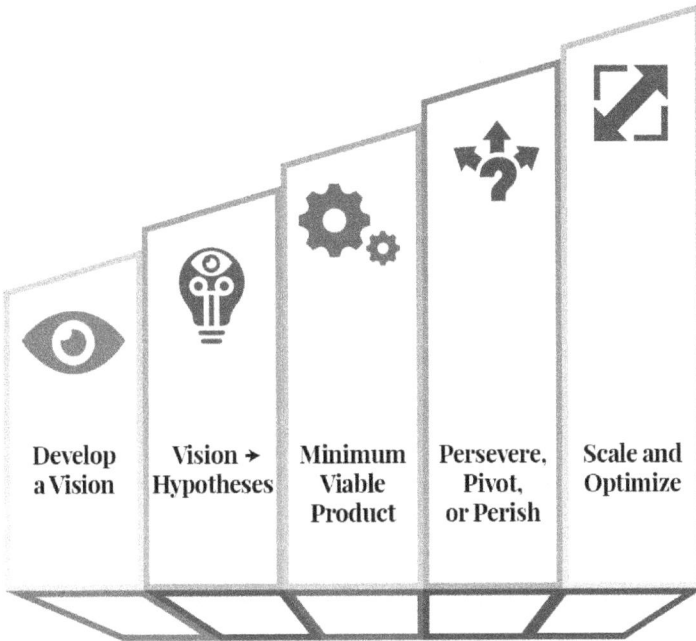

| Develop a Vision | Vision → Hypotheses | Minimum Viable Product | Persevere, Pivot, or Perish | Scale and Optimize |

Stepwise Feasibility Approach

One method to help assess the viability of an entrepreneurial idea is the Stepwise Feasibility Approach, which is comprised of the following steps:

- **Market:** Is there a market for the product or service? Is customer demand high enough to support the idea?

- **Technical:** Is the idea technically plausible? Do we have the capabilities to produce it?

- **Financial:** Is the profit margin worth the risk involved? Is the business model financially viable and sustainable?

- **Competitive**: Is the idea better/faster/cheaper than competitors' products? Is it unique in a way that adds value? What might be the competitive response by rivals when the product or service is released? What barriers to entry and imitation exist to discourage new entrants?

- **Organizational:** What processes and routines are necessary to bring the product or service to market? Are we the right organization to release and manage the new product or service?

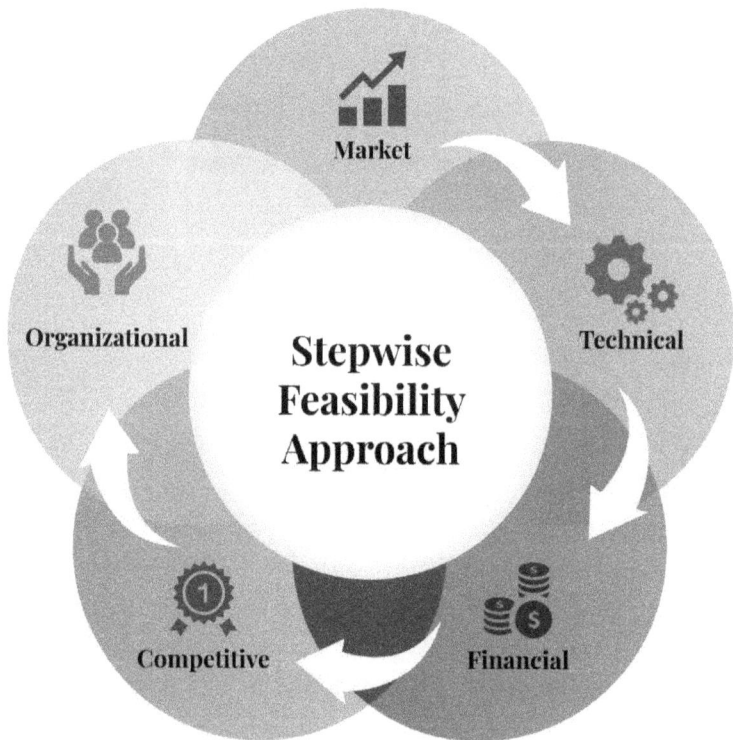

Reflection Question: What's the most important part of the Stepwise Feasibility Approach? Why?

The order of these activities is important. If entrepreneurs are not able to satisfy the first step, namely whether a market even exists for the product or service, then they can stop and don't need to worry about the next step, which is determining if it is actually technically possible. Put another way, it doesn't matter how competitive or financially viable a product or service is if nobody wants to buy it or if the entrepreneur can't build it. Similarly, if competitors are already doing it better, faster, and/or cheaper than the focal firm can do it, it won't matter how effectively organized the startup is.

Even if all of the above areas are positively assessed, one of the most common pitfalls for entrepreneurs is a lack of objective evaluation. Oftentimes, entrepreneurs are so close to their ideas (their "babies") that they are unable to admit flaws or shortcomings, which leads to pursuing an idea that is quite likely to fail. Thus, when evaluating an idea in line with the lean entrepreneurship model, entrepreneurs need to make sure they are being objective and not letting their personal opinions or desires cloud their analyses of their investigations.

Seinfeld Sensei Application

Jerry conducted some market research in order to learn more about relationships, though the endeavor wasn't technically tied to an idea for a new business.

Season 8, Episode 1 "The Foundation" (2:43)

Conducting market research was an excellent way for Jerry to gauge what might work for his primary target audience. Via trial and error and by expending few resources, Jerry applied lean entrepreneurship principles and eventually discovered a successful path to follow.

Kramer came up with an innovative idea to help improve his daily life but needed to conduct some important market research to not only learn more about the problem to be solved but also to test his solution with his potential audience.

Season 9, Episode 9 "The Apology" (4:38)

Even though Kramer's shower disposal idea seemed to have solved his particular problems, the feedback he received from his potential customers was, shall we say, less than positive. That population of potential customers was ostensibly made up of germaphobes, but a reasonable assumption is that this reaction would extrapolate to the general population. Thus, rather than investing important resources in the pursuit of this idea, Kramer could pivot and direct his energies to more lucrative activities.

Chapter 8: Entrepreneurial Adoption

Big Question Question: What difficulties exist for consumers in adopting new entrepreneurial ideas, and how can entrepreneurs overcome these difficulties?

Entrepreneurship is, almost by definition, doing something that has never been done in the exact same way before. Even when demand exists, and the new product or service is something customers want, these same customers might still face obstacles in adopting the new products and services introduced by entrepreneurs. At this point, an important step for entrepreneurs is to put themselves in the minds, hearts, and even wallets of their potential customers to consider what these obstacles might be and how they might help customers overcome them. This chapter is designed to explore some of these obstacles.

Switching Costs

Customers face **switching costs** when they have to pay a price in order to adopt a new product or service. These costs fall into three categories:

(1) financial (exit fees, search costs, compatible equipment); (2) cognitive (learning new ways of doing things); and (3) psychological/emotional (feeling locked in, abandoning existing or creating new personal relation-ships).

Switching Costs

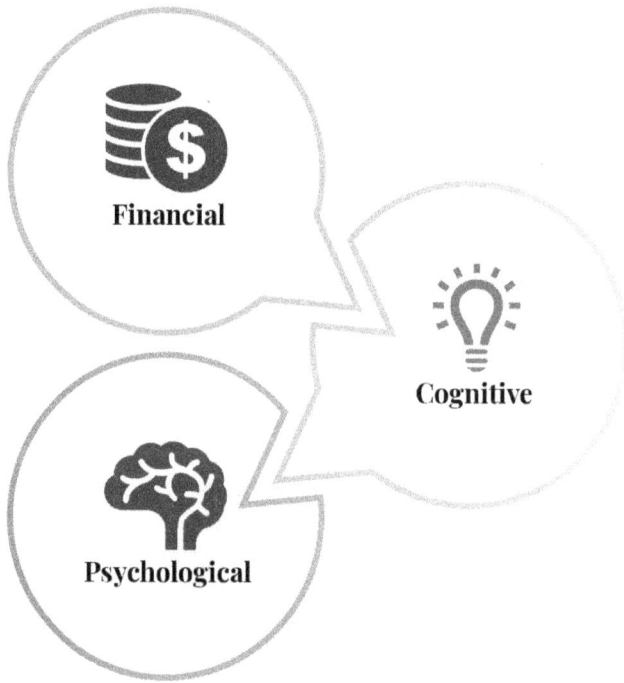

Financial

Cognitive

Psychological

For example, if someone wants to switch from an iPhone to an Android phone, several costs are involved. First, iPhones use a lightning charger, whereas Androids typically use mini-USB or USB-C ports, so a customer wanting a new type of phone would need to invest in a whole new set of chargers. Next, an entirely new operating system has to be learned, with apps that need to be downloaded and installed, including logging back into those accounts, all of which are cognitively taxing activities. Finally, iPhone users who text each other display blue bubbles in their texts, whereas an Android user shows up as a green bubble. Since some iPhone users tend to be somewhat particular (or snooty) about being iPhone users, newly classified green bubble texters could prompt some psychological or emotional adjustment.

Typically, the higher the switching costs, the less likely a new innovation will be adopted. Entrepreneurs, then, should work hard to make initial switching costs low to help increase the likelihood of adoption. But firms can also use switching costs to incentivize their existing customers not to use competitors' products or services. For example, airlines use frequent flyer programs to lock in their customers and to help discourage them from flying with competitors by making it more attractive to accrue benefits with one airline. This dual nature of switching costs must be understood by entrepreneurs to ensure such costs are reduced for new customers but increased for existing customers.

Reflection Question: What particular switching costs can you identify that might impede customers adopting your solution? How might you help them overcome or minimize these costs?

Network Effects

In the case of some products and services, their value increases the more people use them, which can reduce switching costs by helping customers adopt a new product or service. These are known as **network effects** and can be both positive and negative for entrepreneurs. On the positive side, once users adopt the innovation, switching costs can increase for others as the value of being in the network increases, and growth can thus be exponential. Continuing with the airline example above, individual carriers will often partner with other carriers to expand their services and increase the value of their combined frequent flyer programs.

But often a "chicken and egg" dilemma occurs where entrepreneurs need users to attract partners and advertisers but can't attract users until those partners come on board. A primary example of this is eBay, which solidified itself as a dominant online marketplace to bring together buyers and sellers. Without a lot of buyers, sellers would be less motivated to sell their goods on eBay; without many sellers, buyers would be less motivated to search eBay for new items to buy. Early innovation and investment within this space allowed eBay to capitalize on first-mover advantages and build its network to become the standard for online exchanges.

Seinfeld Sensei Application

Kramer had a new idea for a coffee table book and was considerate of his potential customers to make sure they could appreciate what he had to offer. (Note: Some inconsistencies exist with prior iterations of Kramer's idea from episode to episode).

Season 5, Episode 10 "The Cigar Store Indian" and Season 5, Episode 22 "The Opposite" (4:46)

Kramer demonstrated how to anticipate a potential roadblock for adoption. His coffee table book required an actual coffee table to be fully appreciated, so he included a way for customers to transform his book into a coffee table if they didn't have one. In addition, recognizing the problem George had with Jerry leaving a ring from his coffee cup, Kramer decided to include a coaster on the front cover as an added bonus. Unfortunately, Kramer's behavior on his book tour caused him to become the center of his own personal scandal (a topic discussed in the next section), interfering with his continued ability to market his book and consequently inhibiting adoption.

Legal Issues

Legal issues can be a major impediment to adoption, and often young, new firms don't have the necessary resources to deal with these issues on top of other processes necessary for getting their product and company off the ground. Sometimes entrepreneurial firms face fierce resistance by incumbent (already existing) companies that don't want to be disrupted by the new firm. These companies may choose to **lobby** legislatures to enact laws restricting entry and operations in the industry. For example, ride-sharing companies such as Uber and Lyft are facing heavy resistance by taxi and limousine unions and lobbyist groups when they expand to new cities around the world. Other legal challenges, such as **product defects**, introduce liability issues, and the negative reputation from bad press can critically injure new firms, which don't necessarily have the experience or goodwill to overcome such negative perception. Tesla has come under scrutiny for a fatal car crash in which its "autopilot" technology failed to identify an obstacle; hoverboards have caught on fire and exploded, causing damage and initiating recalls and negative perceptions, hurting the adoption of this new product. Finally, **personal scandals**, such as company leaders being indicted for fraud, embezzlement, sexual harassment, and so forth, can derail a young company from being accepted by the marketplace.

Legal Issues and Adoption

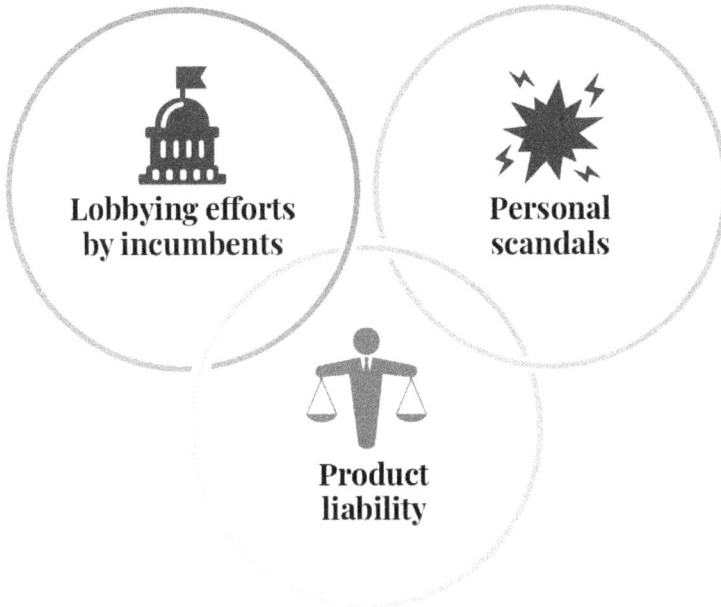

Lobbying efforts by incumbents

Personal scandals

Product liability

Seinfeld Sensei Application

Kramer encountered some issues with a favorite product of his, and he sought help from legal counsel to rectify his situation.

Season 7, Episode 2 "The Postponement" and Season 7, Episode 3 "The Maestro" (4:14)

The coffee company recognized the potentially major negative impact of Kramer having burnt himself with their product. By settling, they avoided damage to their reputation, but young entrepreneurial firms might not be able to afford such an outcome.

Similarly, Kramer experienced the negative and harmful side effects of smoking, and again enlisted the help of his lawyer to receive compensation.

Season 8, Episode 9 "The Abstinence" (3:54)

Product liability can create not only harm to users of the product, but also can damage the company's reputation in the marketplace. For brand new, entrepreneurial firms, this negative reputation can be especially damaging, and can even lead to the end of the firm before it really gets started.

Chapter 9: Entrepreneurial Business Models

Big Question Question: What are the various business models available to entrepreneurs?

A vitally important element of the entrepreneurial process is figuring out how to make money, since a firm's existence isn't sustainable if it isn't able to be profitable. A firm's **business model** consists of strategies, competitive tactics, and initiatives that detail the manner in which the firm will make money. These can come in various forms and can change or evolve over time, but aligning the right business model with the right firm is critical to early success.

Types of business models include:

- **Wholesale/Retail**: manufacturers sell to companies that then resell to customers
- **Direct to consumer**: manufacturers bypass wholesalers/retailers
- **Complementary goods**: firms sell one good at a loss in order to increase sales of another good at a large profit
- **Subscription**: customers pay a fixed amount per period

- **Transactional**: customers pay per use
- **Agent**: a firm relies on an intermediary to sell on its behalf and pays the intermediary a commission
- **Freemium**: a basic version of the product is available for free with advanced functionality requiring payment
- **Bundling**: two or more products are sold together in order to increase overall sales of both
- **Advertisement**: the product or service is given away for free and the firm makes money by selling ads or by selling user information for ads
- **Franchising**: operators pay a fee to open stores based on a concept owned and controlled by another company

Business Models

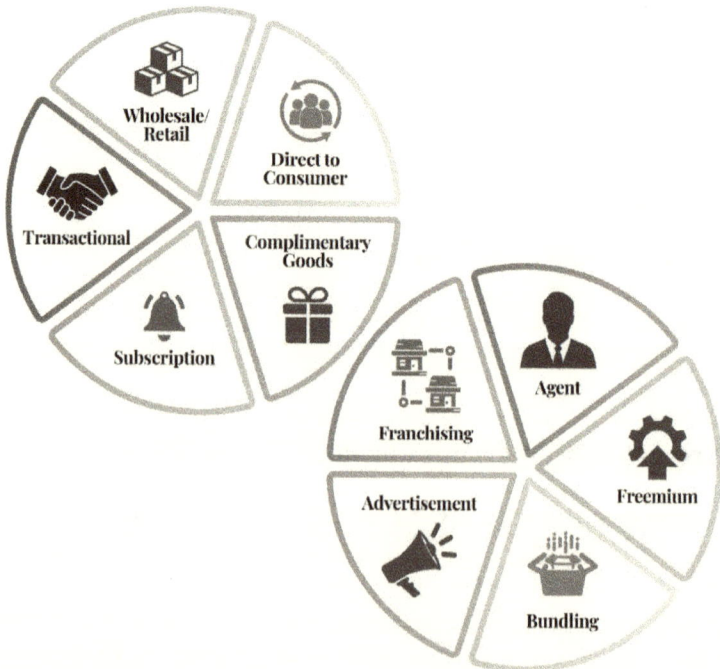

Reflection question: Which of these business model options are particularly attractive for entrepreneurial firms? Which ones might be more difficult to implement for startups?

Keep in mind some of these business models can be used in combination with others, and sometimes **business model innovation** is an area for entrepreneurial opportunities to disrupt current business practices. To be more specific, changing the players involved in the business activities can be a creative and innovative source for new ideas. For example, instead of using traditional taxicab owners or hotels, firms like Uber and Airbnb have revolutionized traditional service industries by simply using people with cars and an extra place to sleep. Other firms, such as Dollar Shave Club, are using technologies like the internet to bypass traditional retail outlets and sell directly to consumers, lowering their costs and leveraging catchy marketing campaigns to outmaneuver more established firms in the marketplace.

Seinfeld Sensei Application

Franchising is often used to help a firm grow because it can leverage its brand to expand into new markets without having to divert too much managerial time and attention and without having to expend its own resources alone to open up new branches. One downside of the franchise model is the lack of managerial control, and actions conducted by one franchisee could damage the reputation of the entire chain.

From a franchisee's perspective, the relative risk of getting into entrepreneurship in this model is low, as the entrepreneur is not required to start an entire firm from scratch and can rely on the established brand to get a jump start. Often these chains meet resistance from local residents who prefer the personal, intimate relationships with mom and pop shops already in existence.

Jerry, Kramer, and local residents reacted to a new chain coming to their neighborhood.

Season 8, Episode 8 "The Chicken Roaster" (4:48)

Although Kenny Rogers Roasters met with some initial resistance, eventually it was accepted, though later some unfortunate incidents caused its demise. Such events might result in a damaged reputation for an entire chain, so franchisors must be diligent when selecting new franchisees and must monitor their activities to ensure the firm is protected from unwanted activities and undesirable outcomes.

Yet another example of a business model is the concept of a royalty, where an entrepreneur licenses a product or service to another firm in exchange for a percentage of their sales.

Season 8, Episode 7 "The Checks" (1:52)

Jerry received hundreds of twelve-cent royalty checks as a result of his brief appearance on a Japanese TV show. Although relinquishing some upside potential from licensing, royalties allow the entrepreneur to also reduce risk and to utilize the notoriety of another entity, in this case the *Super Terrific Happy Hour*, to gain financial success and exposure.

Value Chain

Another important area of discussion in this topic is that of a **value chain**, which describes the activities firms engage in to transform a resource from raw materials to end product. Each link in the chain is designed to improve the product by adding value and making it more attractive to each successive participant in the sequence. Entrepreneurs can capitalize on opportunities along the value chain to disrupt common industry practices and change the way "things have always been done." Innovative ways to reduce the importance or to remove entire parts of the value chain can allow entrepreneurs to enter existing industries and to change conditions in their favor.

Value chain analysis becomes a process of asking and answering the following questions:

1. What are common steps for moving a product from raw materials to the end consumer?
2. What parts of this process create the most value?
3. What parts of the value chain can be exploited, replaced, or disrupted to create an entrepreneurial opportunity?

For example, think of the steps needed to provide a pizza for customers. The primary raw material is seeds (such as corn or alfalfa) cultivated by seed farmers, which are then planted and harvested by crop farmers. The grown plants are then purchased by dairy farmers who feed them to cows, who then process those plants into milk, which is further processed into cheese. The cheese is packaged and sent to food distributors, who sell them to pizza chains, who put the cheese on pizza and sell it to consumers.

Reflection Question: What entrepreneurial opportunities do you see in the above value chain?

What if, for example, instead of milk from cows a creative entrepreneur created a process to use almond milk to make cheese? This type of innovation could remove the current farming process from the equation and help the entrepreneur capture the value from the first few steps of the value chain. This could also help remove one of the most expensive parts of the chain—feeding and maintaining livestock—thereby reducing the overall cost of the process, which could then be passed on to customers in the form of lower prices. Opportunity-seeking entrepreneurs who disrupt the status quo can create solutions to benefit society as a whole as well as themselves.

Seinfeld Sensei Application

Kramer and Newman tried to use their resource advantages to demonstrate how a traditional industry business model could be reshaped for financial success.

Season 7, Episode 20 "The Bottle Deposit" (3:57)

Newman's numerous attempts to solve the Michigan bottle deposit idea proved unsuccessful until he was able to identify a unique resource to which he had access. By disrupting the typical business model of the recycling process, he and Kramer exemplified the entrepreneurial mindset. Continual problem solving and leveraging of unique resources available to them allowed Kramer and Newman to exploit an opportunity in a traditionally difficult financial environment to explore an entrepreneurial venture.

Chapter 10: Entrepreneurial Financing

Big Question Question: What are the possible sources of financial capital available to entrepreneurs?

Entrepreneurial firms are often described as being resource constrained, and one of the most important resources for young firms is **financial capital**. Various sources of financial capital exist, each with advantages and disadvantages, and entrepreneurs must analyze the tradeoffs involved with each funding source.

The two general types of funding are debt and equity. **Debt** is secured or collateralized financing of a new venture that involves a payback of the funds plus a fee, called interest, for the use of the money. **Equity** financing involves the sale or exchange of some of the ownership interest in the venture in return for an unsecured investment in the firm.

Reflection Question: What are the respective pros and cons of debt and equity as sources of capital?

Growth Stage Model

The sources of funding available to entrepreneurial firms often follow a **Growth Stage Model** where founders seek funds dependent upon various milestones and developments within the business.

The first source of funding is usually the **personal funds** of the founder, not only due to ease of access, but also because this practice signals to future investors that the entrepreneur is committed to and optimistic about the outcome of the firm. A heavy financial commitment can also help motivate the entrepreneur to work hard and to focus on the long-term financial viability of the venture. The next source of financial capital often comes from the entrepreneur's **friends and family** (sometimes playfully referred to as friends, family, and fools), who are typically individuals closely acquainted with the founding entrepreneur(s) and fund new firms based on this relationship, rather than on the underlying merits of the business itself. Friends and family have been shown to provide needed validation and social support for the founder, but because friends and family members may lack business experience or expertise relevant to the new firm, they are often unable to offer additional managerial or strategic advice to the entrepreneur. Moreover, they may base their decisions on the entrepreneur's optimism when it comes to assessing the likelihood of the new firm's success rather than conducting their own due diligence on the underlying potential of the firm.

Investor Classes by Funding Stage

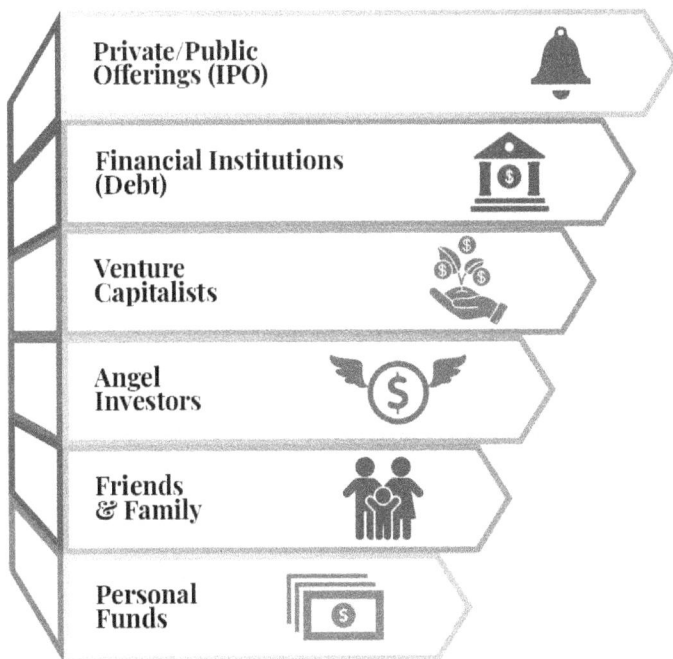

Private/Public Offerings (IPO)
Financial Institutions (Debt)
Venture Capitalists
Angel Investors
Friends & Family
Personal Funds

Angel Investors

The next source of funding often comes from **angel investors**, who are wealthy individuals investing their own money in early stage ventures. They usually expect an ownership equity stake in exchange for financial capital and are often concerned with giving back to a local community or a member of a group to which they have ties (such as an alma mater).

Angels tend to invest in smaller-sized deals (usually up to half a million dollars) and expect to make a modest profit with a payback period of five to seven years. They can also help provide some guidance based on their experience to help the entrepreneur develop the startup. On the downside, because angels tend to be locally situated, they can't usually provide a national image or widespread connections for future leverage. They also tend to not offer follow-on investments as the startup grows and needs additional capital.

Reflection Question: Who in your personal network might be a good source of financial capital and advice for your growing business?

Venture Capitalists

The next step for equity investments are typically **venture capitalists** (VCs), who are professional investors. VCs collect money from wealthy individuals or institutional investors and pool this money to create funds, from which they invest in entrepreneurial firms, expecting a large return on this investment (often ten times the amount of capital invested) in a relatively short period of time, usually three to five years. VCs tend to invest in certain industries in which they have particular experience and expertise and are often able to offer value beyond simply money in the form of social/professional connections (with lawyers, accountants, customers, potential distribution network partners, and so forth), strategic advice, and high reputational spillovers. In addition to equity, VCs often require a seat or several seats on the firm's board of directors, from which they are able to weigh in on strategic decisions such as hiring and firing the top management team and entering into large contracts. VCs often require sophisticated business plans and heavily scrutinize the firm both in terms of the plan and, if the firm passes the initial screening of the plan, during a formal presentation.

Financial Institutions (Debt)

Debt financing often comes from **financial institutions** such as commercial banks, government agencies, or the Small Business Association (SBA), which makes one- to five-year intermediate-term loans secured by collateral from the business, including receivables, inventories, and other assets. Early in the life of the firm, this debt is collateralized by the personal assets of the founder (house, car, credit cards) because the firm does not have much in the form of valuable assets that can be used as collateral. The value of this collateral is important to commercial banks because if the firm should go bankrupt or be unable to pay the regular interest due, the bank receives the collateral and sells it to help cover the amount of the loan. This is typically known as a "fire sale," where the value of company assets is greatly discounted, and the bank is often only able to receive about 50 percent of book value. Although debt financing is typically cheaper than equity from a weighted perspective, and the lenders don't require relinquishment of ownership or board seats, the biggest downside is the regular interest payments required on the loan. Since entrepreneurial firms are filled with risk and uncertainty, especially if and when sales are to be made to new or nonexistent customers, the receipt of cash can be irregular. But what is absolutely known is that periodic interest payments are due, and this mismatch of cash flows can be financially ruinous for startups.

Private and Public Offerings

The remaining equity markets come in the form of **private placements**, wherein a select group of investors purchase shares in the firm, and an **initial public offering** (IPO), during which the stock market at large is able to purchase shares of stock in the company. For VCs and other early investors, the largest payoff usually comes when a firm goes public with an IPO. IPOs can generate a lot of wealth and notoriety for entrepreneurial firms and can create liquidity for trading the firms' stocks. The downsides of public offerings include the cost of the IPO process, the disclosure requirements for publicly traded firms, and increased shareholder pressure going forward.

Reflection Question: What are the advantages and disadvantages of each source of funding for entrepreneurial ventures? Which one might be best for you at your stage of entrepreneurial development?

One important difference between debt and equity is what the entrepreneur is giving up when borrowing these funds. With banks, usually no advice or guidance is given (what is referred to as "dumb money") and regular interest payments in an uncertain world are expected. With equity, the entrepreneurs are literally giving up a portion of the business they've worked so hard to create, but in return equity investors are often able to use their experience, expertise, and connections to provide mentoring and guidance. Because the financier is now a part owner of the firm, however, some disagreement can exist between the financier and the entrepreneur regarding the strategic direction of the firm.

Seinfeld Sensei Application

Kramer first reached out to some friends for a financial investment to start his entrepreneurial venture but ultimately settled on an angel investor.

Season 1, Episode 4 "The Male Unbonding" and Season 6, Episode 5 "The Couch" (3:33)

Kramer and Poppie disagreed about how Kramer's initial idea might be implemented in practice. Since Poppie had provided vital financial capital and had extensive relevant industry experience, perhaps he felt a bit entitled to give that advice and expected Kramer to listen to him, even when his ideas deviated from Kramer's initial vision. Another interesting principle in this example is how much the reputation of the entrepreneur and the investor become intertwined, for better or for worse. Jerry pointed out that Poppie had gotten in trouble with the Board of Health, and this negative reputation spillover could have harmed Kramer's idea. Of course the entrepreneur's status can also be elevated if the investor has a positive reputation, so entrepreneurs must weigh the pros and cons of partnering with investors, a decision which can make or break the success of the firm.

Angels and venture capitalists will often only interact with people whom they either know personally or who are referred to them by a trusted source. George demonstrated how knowing someone on the "inside" was often an initial hurdle to being included in the rest of the process.

Season 8, Episode 3 "The Bizarro Jerry" (4:17)

George was able to establish his legitimacy by having a key network connection to gain access to the "Forbidden City." Of course, what happens once access is gained is up to the entrepreneur.

Chapter 11: Entrepreneurial Planning

Big Question Question: What are the essential elements of business planning? How do entrepreneurs plan in such an uncertain world?

A **business plan** is a document that lays out the various elements of the entrepreneurial firm centered around a main idea or primary solution to a perceived problem or opportunity. It describes the current status, expected needs, and projected results of the new business. A complete business plan covers the major elements needed to implement the idea and presents guidelines for a successful enterprise. Business plans provide needed information to various stakeholders, especially potential investors who use it as a mechanism for evaluation.

Benefits of Planning

One of the main benefits of a business plan is that it forces entrepreneurs to view their venture critically and objectively with close **scrutiny**. When one has to write something down, it forces deeper thought and raises the bar for clarity; this is more productive than keeping it all in one's head. By asking and answering the critical questions necessary to writing a complete business plan, entrepreneurs become experts in the industry and the environment in which they intend to do business and gain a much deeper and **holistic understanding** of multiple facets of the venture. Writing a business plan also forces entrepreneurs to **quantify** objectives, goals, benchmarks, and assumptions, all of which need to be validated as the plan unfolds. When shared with those inside the organization, the plan becomes a **roadmap** for employees and other internal stakeholders. And when shared with those outside the firm, it becomes the main **communication tool** between the firm and financial providers, potential employees, strategic partners, and so forth. Although the plan will continue to change and evolve, the planning process is crucial to the current and long-term success of the entrepreneurial venture.

The key concept is for entrepreneurs to continually learn and to update the business plan accordingly. In this way, the business plan itself remains relevant and the business planning process helps entrepreneurs make sure they are staying aware and taking advantage of the changing circumstances around them.

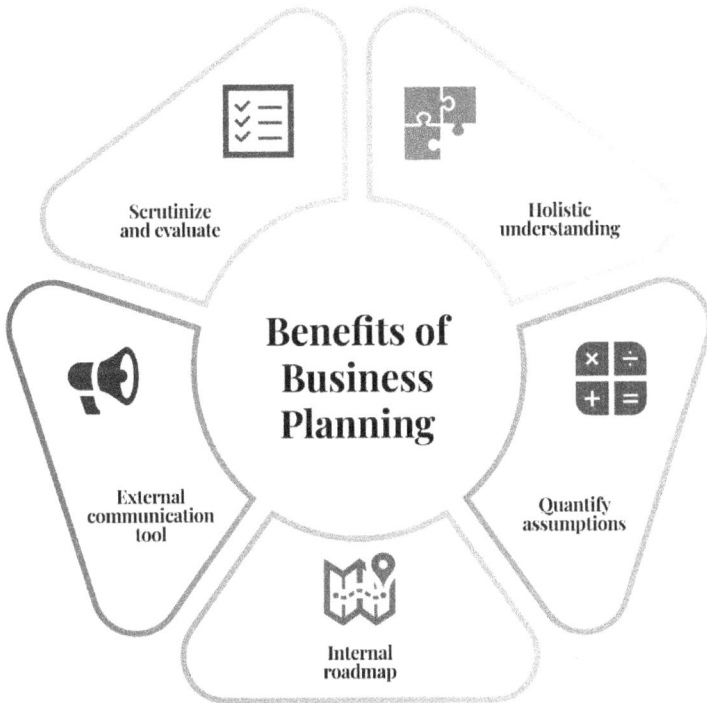

Benefits of Business Planning

- Scrutinize and evaluate
- Holistic understanding
- Quantify assumptions
- Internal roadmap
- External communication tool

Seinfeld Sensei Application

Kramer and Newman demonstrated what can happen when founders don't think through the key operations and critical risks of a new venture.

Season 9, Episode 17 "The Bookstore" (3:02)

Kramer and Newman failed to consider key human resource and operational activities (who would do what) and allowed someone else to control the key resources of the business.

Business Model Canvas

The **Business Model Canvas** (BMC) is a recent addition to the entrepreneurial planning process and the tools available for helping entrepreneurs. It acts as a template to help entrepreneurs visualize their ideas and streamline the business planning process to help develop and document new or existing business models. Although *business* is included in the name, this roadmap can be used for almost any project or idea: a family-owned business, a technology business, a nonprofit organization, a social venture, existing businesses, new businesses, etc. The BMC is a central planning tool that helps provide the framework for many of the things entrepreneurs need to know before and while a business or organization is being built. The visual chart on the next page includes elements to help the entrepreneur explore the firm's value proposition, infrastructure, customers, partners, and finances.

To create a Business Model Canvas for their ideas, entrepreneurs make best guesses (hypotheses) as to how the business or organization will work. The entrepreneur then becomes a scientist and tests those guesses by interacting with potential customers and other key stakeholders who will help refine the idea. Using the information gained during these interactions, the BMC is then updated, often many times, to reflect increasingly better understanding of the firm's or organization's role. Because a market is dynamic, the BMC should be updated based on changes in customer preferences, trends, competitor responses, partnership arrangements, and so forth. The BMC might also be updated based on changes in goals or expectations initiated by the entrepreneurs or to reflect changes in understanding or experience as the entrepreneurs learns more about their market and idea.

Simplified Business Model Canvas

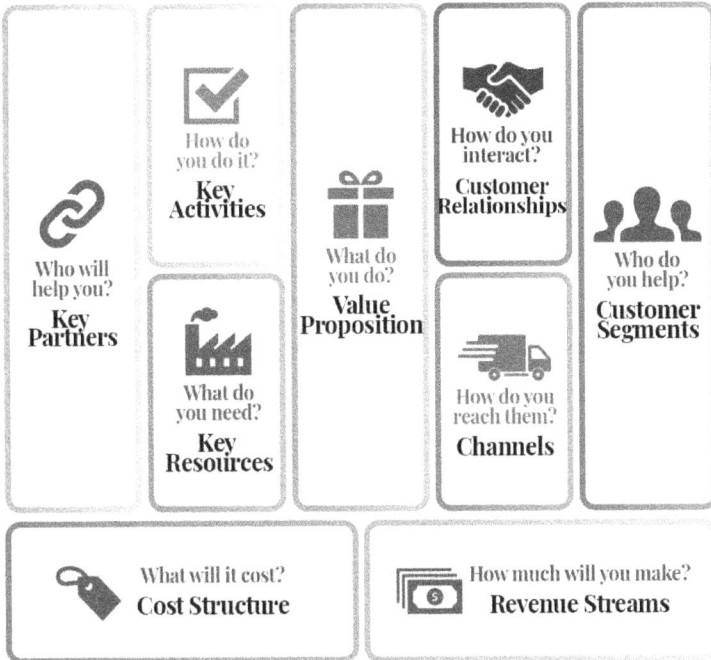

Reflection Question: Where do you think the best place to start planning your entrepreneurial idea might be—within which box do you think you should start?

Some more specific information and questions for each section include the following:

- **Customer Segments:** the groups of people for whom value is created. This section answers questions such as: Who are our most important customers? What are the customer archetypes/personas? What are the demographic, psychographic, and behavioral characteristics of our primary target audience?

- **Value Proposition:** the value added or created for the customer. This section addresses questions such as: Which of our customers' problems are we helping to solve? What bundles of products and services are we offering to each segment? Which customer needs are we satisfying? What is the minimum viable product?

- **Customer Relationships:** the kinds of relationships you have with each of your customer segments and how you communicate with them. This section answers questions such as: How do we attract, keep, and grow customers? Which customer relationships have we established? How are they integrated with the rest of our business model? How costly are they? How do we inform and learn from our customers?

- **Customer Channels** (sometimes referred to as Distribution Channels): the ways your product will reach your customer segments. This section addresses questions such as: Through which channels do our customer segments want to be reached? How do other companies reach them now? Which ones work best? Which ones are most cost-efficient? How are we integrating them with customer routines?

- **Key Activities:** the things you'll need to do to make your value proposition, channels, relationships, and revenue streams happen. This section answers the following questions: What key activities do our value propositions require? What about our distribution channels? Customer relationships? Revenue streams?

- **Key Resources:** all the important elements you will need to fulfill your value proposition, channels, relationships, and revenue streams. The following questions are addressed in this section: What key resources do our value propositions require? And our distribution channels? Customer relationships? Revenue streams?

- **Key Partners:** the people or organizations you will need to work with to complete key activities and to access key resources. This section considers the following questions: Who are our key partners? Who are our key suppliers? Which key resources are we acquiring from our partners? What are the key activities that partners perform?

- **Cost Structure:** the costs associated with your key resources and activities. This section explores questions such as: What are the most important costs inherent to your business model? Which key resources are most expensive? Which key activities are most expensive?

- **Revenue Streams:** how and how much your customers will pay for the value you provide. This section will answer the following questions: For what type of value are our customers willing to pay? For what do they currently pay? What is the revenue model? What are the pricing tactics?

Reflection question: What important element(s) might be missing from the current Business Model Canvas?

Missing Components

Two key elements are missing from the above BMC. The first is **competition**, where understanding who competitors are, what competitors are currently doing (or planning to do), and how they may or may not be satisfying the needs of customers are critical components of ensuring entrepreneurs' business activities create, deliver, and capture value. In addition, predicting and planning for how competitors might respond is imperative so the negative impact of those rival responses can be minimized.

The second major element overlooked by the current BMC is **critical risks**, which highlight what might go wrong and how such shortcomings will be overcome. All business ventures face risks, but a conscientious entrepreneur will be able to prioritize three to five risks that could be particularly impactful for the new venture. Rather than pretending their venture is invincible, entrepreneurs should acknowledge these critical risks in order to demonstrate they can objectively evaluate their business and are not naïve or untrustworthy.

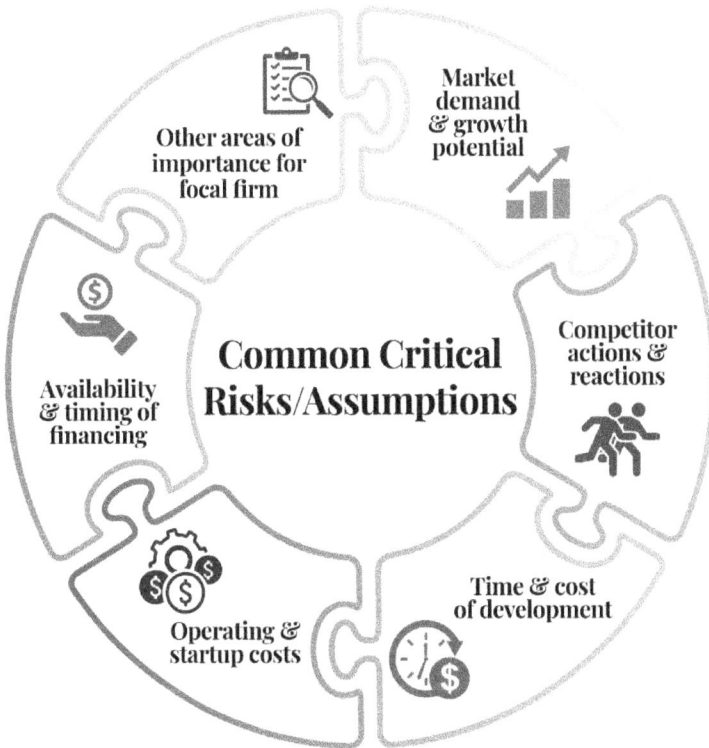

Common categories of critical risks include:

- The size of **market demand and growth potential** (one of the biggest risks a new venture faces is the possibility that, after production, no one buys it)
- **Competitor actions and reactions** (anticipating potential responses)
- The **time and cost involved in developing** the new product or service (outsourcing could help reduce uncertainty)
- **Regular operating and startup expenses** needed (easy for an inexperienced entrepreneur to underestimate costs)
- The **availability and timing of future financing** vital for further growth and development (missing or misunderstanding key milestones)
- Any **other area of particular importance** to the focal firm.

Identifying these critical risks is only the beginning, however, and the most important part of this process involves generating mitigating strategies to minimize the impact these critical risks might have. A risk identified without a mitigating strategy is incomplete and instead creates a reason for stakeholders not to be involved with the new venture.

SenSei

Seinfeld Sensei Application

Elaine and her former boss, Mr. Lippman, encountered some issues when starting a business based on Elaine's idea for a new way to eat muffins.

Season 8, Episode 21 "The Muffin Tops" (4:22)

Mr. Lippman's inability to consider the various aspects of the business—marketing, operations, critical risks—before charging ahead with business operations created problems he couldn't solve on his own. Even some of the solutions presented by Elaine caused additional problems that ultimately required Newman's help to solve. This situation also highlights the danger of making assumptions: Elaine just assumed homeless shelters would welcome the muffin stumps without validating that assumption. Although nobody can perfectly predict the future, entrepreneurs must think through and validate key parts of the business, including planning for what might go wrong to mitigate critical risks that can derail a new startup.

Chapter 12: Entrepreneurial Pitching

Big Question Question: How do entrepreneurs effectively and safely present their ideas to obtain necessary resources?

Salesmanship is often an important characteristic for an entrepreneur, and the ability to persuade others of the potential of a new idea cannot be overlooked. Talking to potential customers is also an effective way to get feedback when testing an idea. In addition, entrepreneurs will often be required to present or "pitch" their idea and business plan to potential resource providers during the funding process.

Criteria for Evaluation

One purpose of pitching an entrepreneurial idea is gaining access to financial capital. Although resource providers will conduct their own due diligence, the responsibility falls on entrepreneurs and their teams to convince them their idea is worth an investment.

Criteria for Evaluation

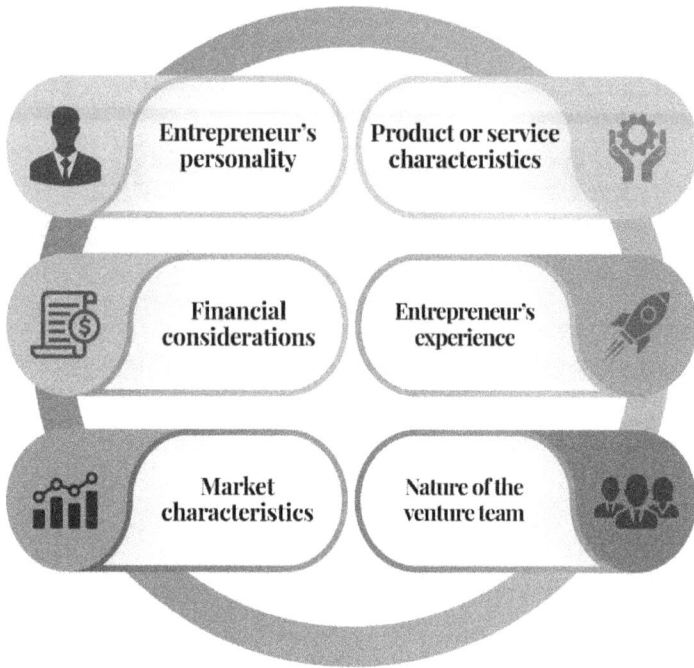

Typically, when evaluating an entrepreneurial idea for funding, potential resource providers look at the following criteria:

- **Entrepreneur's personality** (teachability and amenability)
- **Entrepreneur's experience** (relevant expertise and connections)
- **Product or service characteristics** (better, faster, cheaper than other offerings)
- **Market characteristics** (size, room for growth, accessibility, competitive dynamics)
- **Financial considerations** (profitability, payback period, return on investment)
- **Nature of the venture team** (compatibility, ability to adapt and to

The Startup of Seinfeld

work together)

Elevator Pitch

Rather than a formal presentation with slides and other graphics, sometimes entrepreneurs are faced with a situation where only a short time is available. In this case, an **elevator pitch** is most appropriate. The genesis of this concept comes from a situation where someone is alone in an elevator with an important person and only has the duration of the elevator ride to present an idea to that person. In this case, entrepreneurs have to make sure they capture the attention of the listener, concisely emphasize the most important aspects of the idea, and initiate a call to action to discuss the opportunity at another, more convenient time.

The most effective and **memorable hooks** to grab the attention of the listener come in the form of a question, a story, or a meaningful statistic. If the entrepreneur can help listeners relate to the problem of the target customer, they will be more likely to be engaged and stay interested in hearing more. This also helps the entrepreneur **focus on the pain** or problem to be solved, and can lead quickly into the **value proposition**. Sometimes, using another firm or business model as an example can help the listener understand more quickly the idea or the value proposition, but these comparisons need to be chosen wisely so as not to confuse the listener and to make sure the entrepreneur's idea is better, faster, and/or cheaper than existing alternatives. The end of the pitch should include a **call to action**, such as providing contact information, an invitation to meet again to discuss further, a referral for a customer or resource provider, and so forth. Truncated pitches of **various lengths** can also be prepared so entrepreneurs can effectively present their idea to multiple audiences in different situations.

Elevator Pitch

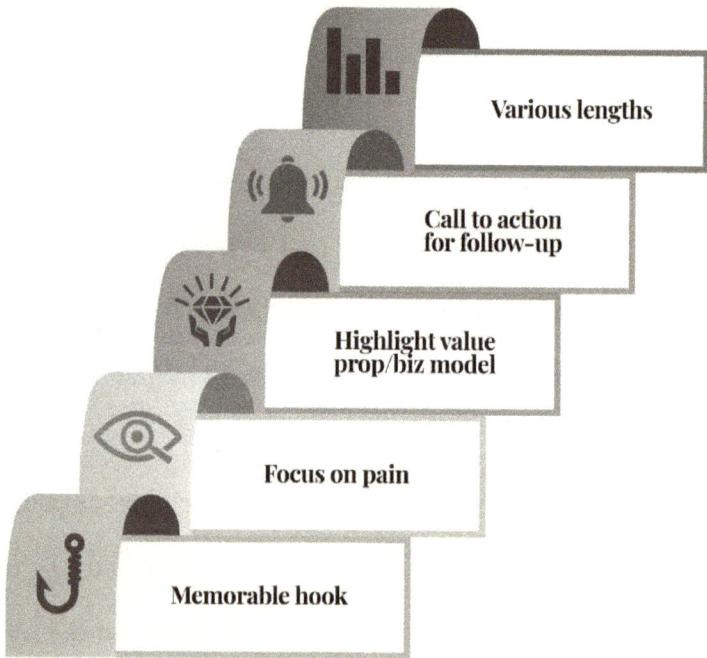

Various lengths

Call to action for follow-up

Highlight value prop/biz model

Focus on pain

Memorable hook

Reflection Question: In what different situations might an elevator pitch be used? What information could be added to ensure the entrepreneur is prepared to discuss the idea for varying lengths of time?

Seinfeld Sensei Application

Jerry taught George the value of showmanship when presenting to an audience, which George was able to use both at work and in his personal life.

Season 9, Episode 16 "The Burning" (4:38)

Often, an audience will remember the last thing you tell them, so ending with a strong call to action that motivates them to engage with you further is an effective technique. Unfortunately, George had the old "switcheroo" played on him and learned what was good for the goose was good for the gander.

Protecting the Idea

Although pitching is an integral part of the entrepreneurial process, a danger exists when pitching an idea that it might be stolen by the listener. Of course the hope is for others to be ethical, but not everybody fits this ideal. Several options are available to entrepreneurs to help guard against this.

Among these options are formal mechanisms:

1. **Nondisclosure agreements** where parties agree not to discuss or otherwise disclose any proprietary information shared between the two parties.

2. **Noncompete agreements** where parties agree that after separation they are not allowed to work for a competitor for a specified period of time.

3. Other **confidentiality** and **intellectual property agreements**, which are covered in more detail in the next chapter.

Formal Mechanisms

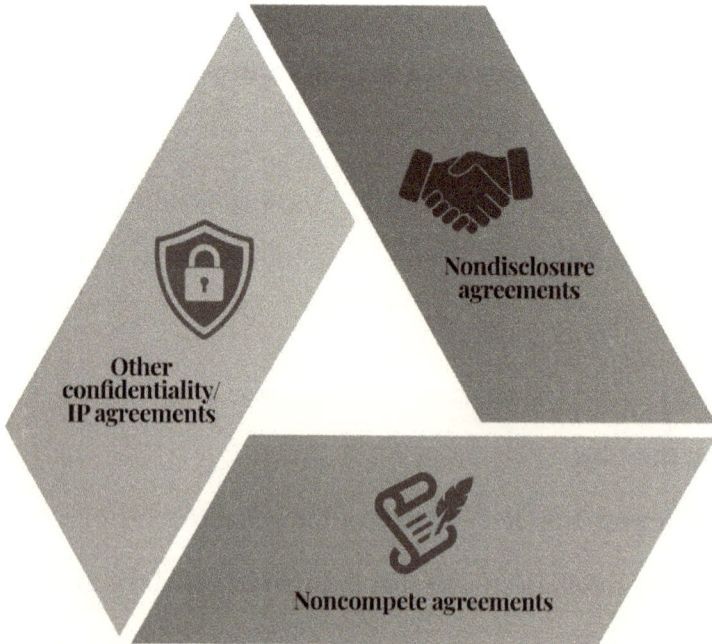

Other confidentiality/ IP agreements

Nondisclosure agreements

Noncompete agreements

Reflection Question: How could your firm benefit from formal mechanisms to protect your ideas?

Other, informal mechanisms can also be used:

1. Focus discussion on the pain (**problem** to be solved) rather than the solution so the listener can't obtain valuable insight into the entrepreneurial idea.

2. Be **vague** about the solution and don't give away the source of competitive advantage or "secret sauce" of the idea.

3. Get a **head start**, so even if listeners do steal the idea, they will have a hard time catching up.

4. Be aware of the **relative resource (competitive) position**, so someone with the resources to quickly and easily imitate the idea won't be able to do so ahead of the entrepreneur.

5. Understand the **nature of the relationship** with whom the idea is being shared, so untrustworthy or unknown parties are not privy to the details of the idea.

Informal Mechanisms

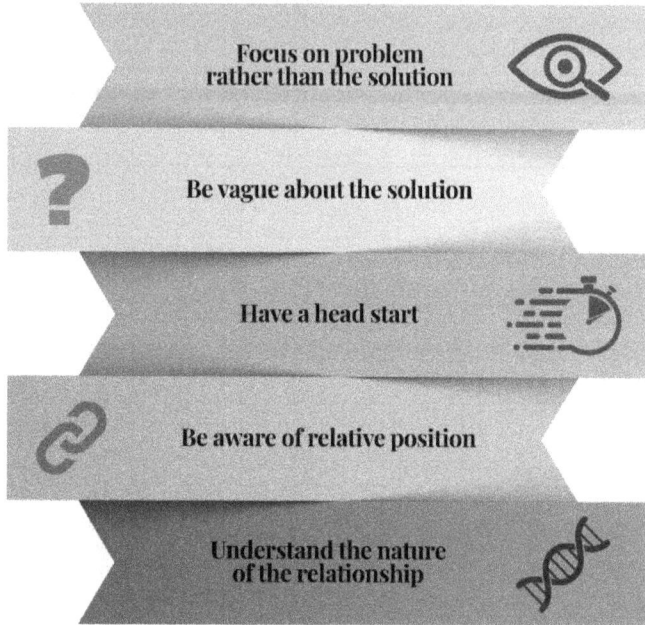

- Focus on problem rather than the solution
- Be vague about the solution
- Have a head start
- Be aware of relative position
- Understand the nature of the relationship

Reflection Question: Have you ever felt your idea was in danger of being stolen? How could the above mechanisms help you protect your ideas while still benefitting from receiving valuable feedback and making important connections?

Seinfeld Sensei Application

Kramer had an idea for a new type of cologne, which he got from his personal experience. He encountered some mixed results as he attempted to explore the possibilities of turning this idea into a reality.

Season 3, Episode 14 "The Pez Dispenser" and Season 4, Episode 13 "The Pick" (4:26)

Kramer's pitching technique had both positive elements and areas in which he could improve. He did a great job sharing a personal and relatable story about going to the beach, but shoving his arm in the faces of his audience could turn some people off. Something to learn from Kramer's experience is to be especially cognizant of one's relative resource position. Although getting feedback from someone who is already in the industry is a great way to receive knowledgeable advice, a company like Calvin Klein is much better situated than Kramer to manufacture and produce a new cologne. Kramer's relationship with the executive also didn't seem strong enough for him to be trusted with a new idea. Perhaps a more effective method would have been for Kramer to create an inexpensive version of his cologne and then present it to Calvin Klein for manufacturing, distribution, or licensing; he could also have entered into a formal agreement to manufacture the cologne without disclosing the scent until after the agreement had been signed. Although Calvin Klein does seem to come to some sort of an alternative arrangement for Kramer's services (not shown), he still missed out on being a fragrance millionaire!

Chapter 13: Intellectual Property Protection

Big Question Question: What legal options do entrepreneurs have to protect their intellectual property?

As entrepreneurs begin to develop their product or service, **intellectual property,** defined as a work or invention that is the result of creativity to which one has rights, is often created. This intellectual property can be the source of much value to the young entrepreneurial firm, but as the firm becomes more and more successful, competitors will begin to take notice. If the intellectual property is not protected, it can simply be imitated or used without permission or compensation, which can reduce or remove the firm's competitive advantage. To help protect intellectual property, several options are available:

1. Patent
2. Trademark
3. Copyright
4. Trade secret

Each one of these options will be explored further throughout this chapter.

Intellectual Property Protection

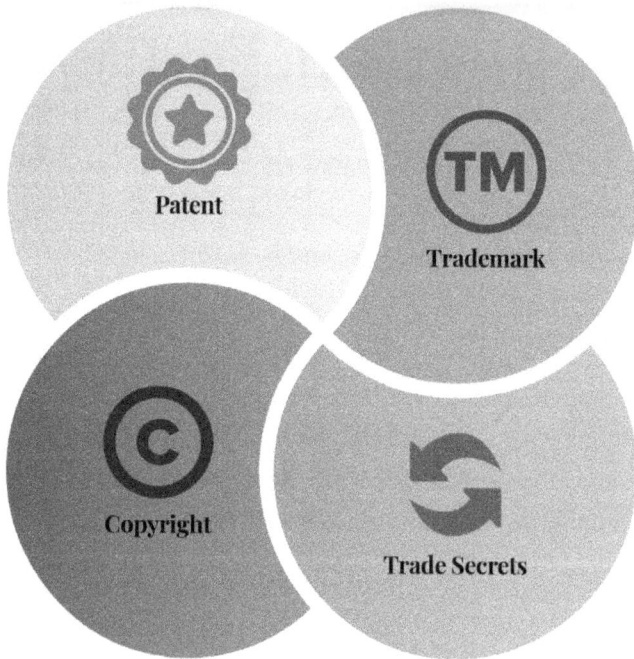

One important caveat to keep in mind is that legal matters are often a matter of subjectivity, where one legal audience might have an opinion not shared by another. Furthermore, certain intellectual property protections might have jurisdictional considerations: Different places have different rules, and some legal protections might not be enforceable outside certain geographical areas.

Patent

When entrepreneurs have an invention or have created something new, they might want to use a **patent** to protect the intellectual property at the foundation of that creation. The United States Patent and Trademark Office (PTO) reviews patent applications and enforces patents once they have been granted. Ownership of a patent allows the creator to prevent someone else from making, using, and/or selling the invention. Only the inventor is allowed to apply for a patent, and if more than one person is involved in the creation of the invention, all participants are required to be included in the same patent. Merely making a financial contribution to the invention process does not qualify the investor to be an inventor and thus an owner of the patent.

Although many different types of patents exist, the two most common are the design patent and the utility patent. A design patent protects the appearance or ornamental design of an invention. Although the application process is generally simpler, and design patents are more likely to be accepted by the PTO, they are usually easier for imitators to circumvent by making modest changes to the design of a product. In order to receive a design patent, the inventor must satisfy two criteria: it must have a new, original, and/or ornamental design, and the novel features of the invention must not be obvious. Design patents are enforceable for fourteen years.

Utility patents protect the function, use, or method of the invention. The inventor must describe how the invention will be used, and thus this type of patent is more complicated, expensive, and extensive than a design patent. As a result, however, the utility patent is often more enforceable because it covers the use or function of an invention, a generally broader and stronger concept. Utility patents are enforceable for twenty years, and most inventions can be filed as a design patent, a utility patent, or both.

Patent

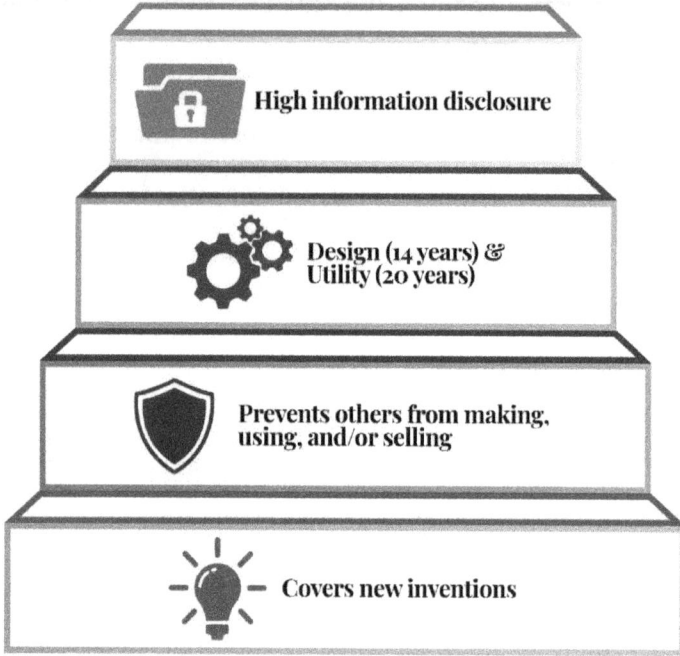

- High information disclosure
- Design (14 years) & Utility (20 years)
- Prevents others from making, using, and/or selling
- Covers new inventions

The PTO uses the following criteria for evaluating utility patent applications:

1. Statutory-class test: The invention must reasonably be classified as a process, machine, manufacture, composition, or a "new use" of one or more of these classifications.

2. Utility test: The invention must be considered useful.

3. Novelty test: The invention needs to have a feature that sets it apart from previous inventions and is unknown to the public.

4. "Unobviousness" test: The invention must not be obvious to some-

one with ordinary skill in the area of the invention. For example, if the invention has something to do with a toothbrush, the uniqueness of the utility can't be considered obvious by someone who uses a toothbrush regularly.

Patent Application Criteria

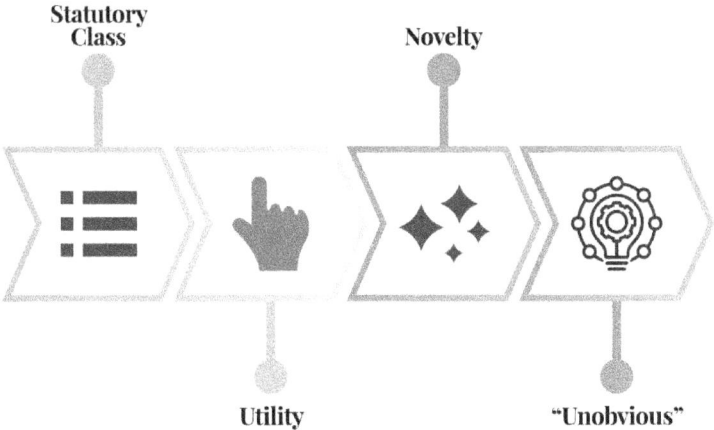

Statutory Class

Novelty

Utility

"Unobvious"

As part of the patent application process, the inventor should demonstrate the product's uniqueness, which usually requires some sort of patent search to ensure no other inventor has already claimed a patent on the design or utility. If the invention relied on a previously granted patent or patents, this fact needs to be listed on the patent application, and the inventor must explain how the new invention is sufficiently different from the referents.

Reflection Question: Can you think of businesses that use patents to protect their intellectual property? How effective do you think this protection mechanism is?

Seinfeld Sensei Application

One criticism of patents focuses on how much information needs to be disclosed in the application. Particularly for utility patents, the inventor needs to describe in detail how the invention is made and its intended uses in the marketplace. Granted patents are part of the public domain (in part so effective searches for later patents can be done), so competitors can learn how a product is produced and how the inventor plans to use it. If those competitors then made changes to the original design or utility of the patented product, they would no longer be in violation of the patent, and the protection that patent provides would be severely compromised.

The Soup Nazi learned the hard way about how the public disclosure of proprietary information could harm his business.

Season 7, Episode 6 "The Soup Nazi" (4:19)

Although the Soup Nazi had probably never filed a patent for his soup recipes, because Elaine now had knowledge of the recipes and the source of his competitive advantage, she threatened to publish them and damage his success. Entrepreneurs need to make sure they protect their proprietary intellectual property.

Trademark

When entrepreneurs want to protect a recognizable design, sign, or expression that uniquely identifies products or services, a **trademark** is most appropriate. A trademark can be granted to an individual, a business organization, or any legal entity. Trademarks are often used to distinguish one firm's products or services from another and as such a trademark from a particular company can signify quality, dependability, or uniqueness relative to other competitors' products. Trademarks are assigned to one of forty-five classes to specify and limit the protection of the intellectual property, and, with only a few exceptions, identifying marks in one category cannot be protected in another category. Terms such as mark, brand, or logo are sometimes used interchangeably with trademark, but the latter also includes any device, brand, label, name, signature, word, letter, numerical, shape of goods, packaging, color or combination of colors, smell, sound, movement, or any combination thereof that allows for the distinguishing of goods and services of one business from another.

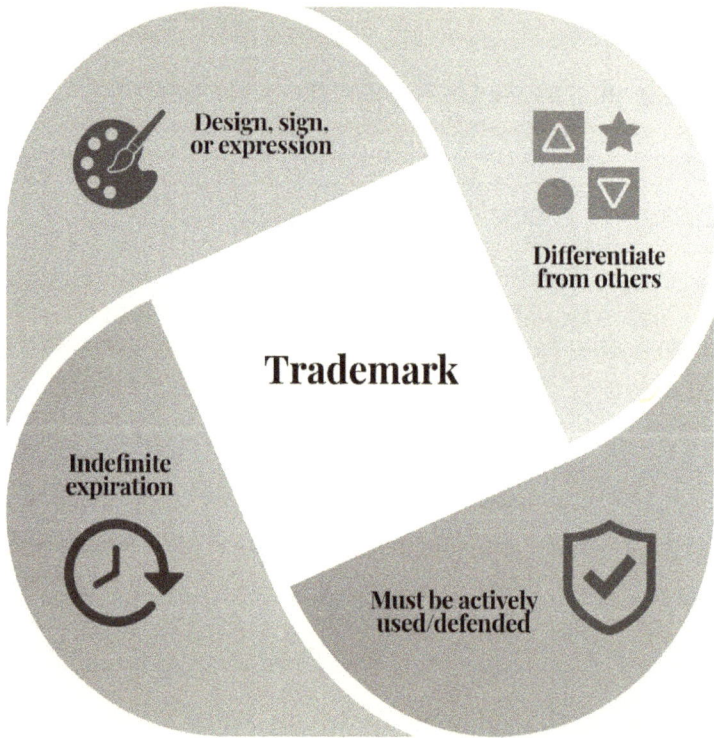

Trademarks must be used in order to retain the rights of protection, usually within a period of five years. In this way, as long as a trademark is actively used and/or defended within this time frame, it can theoretically last forever.

Reflection Question: What's the most valuable trademark you can think of? Have you ever considered trademarking a phrase, statement, or brand?

Seinfeld Sensei Application

The lack of distinguishing important characteristics from one party to another can have disastrous consequences. Elaine's boyfriend Kurt found from personal experience the downside of being mistaken for someone else.

Season 8, Episode 11 "The Little Jerry" (4:41)

In practice, George would have been the one to file a trademark to protect his unique image (even though baldness is hardly unique), but the idea of distinguishing characteristics to prevent others from mistaking one party from another is evident. In business, if customers or other interested stakeholders are unable to distinguish one company's intellectual property from another, the value and subsequent advantage this intellectual property provides could be eroded.

Case in point, George desired to create a nickname for himself to increase his perceived value in the eyes of others, but was unable to adequately protect this nickname before someone else took it away from him.

Season 9, Episode 19 "The Maid" (4:29)

Without any legal protection for his nickname, George had no recourse when a co-worker started going by the desired nickname. Unhappy with the alternate nickname his boss gave to him, George had to come up with other non-legal ways to try to shed this nickname. Had George trademarked T-bone to begin with, he might have been able to avoid the dreaded Koko moniker.

Copyright

For original literary (poems, theses, plays), artistic (paintings, drawings, sculptures, or photographs), musical (compositions, sound recordings, radio and television broadcasts), or other creative works (motion pictures, choreography, computer software, and industrial designs), a **copyright** can be issued to help protect the work from unauthorized use. The copyright owner effectively has exclusive right to:

- reproduce the original work,
- create derivative or spinoff work based on the original, and
- sell, perform, and/or display the copyrighted work in public.

Typically, the person who originally created the work is considered the owner of the copyright, and joint authorship is possible for work created by more than one author. Usually no formal process is required to be covered by a copyright; simply fixing the work in a "tangible form of expression" for the first time establishes ownership of that work.

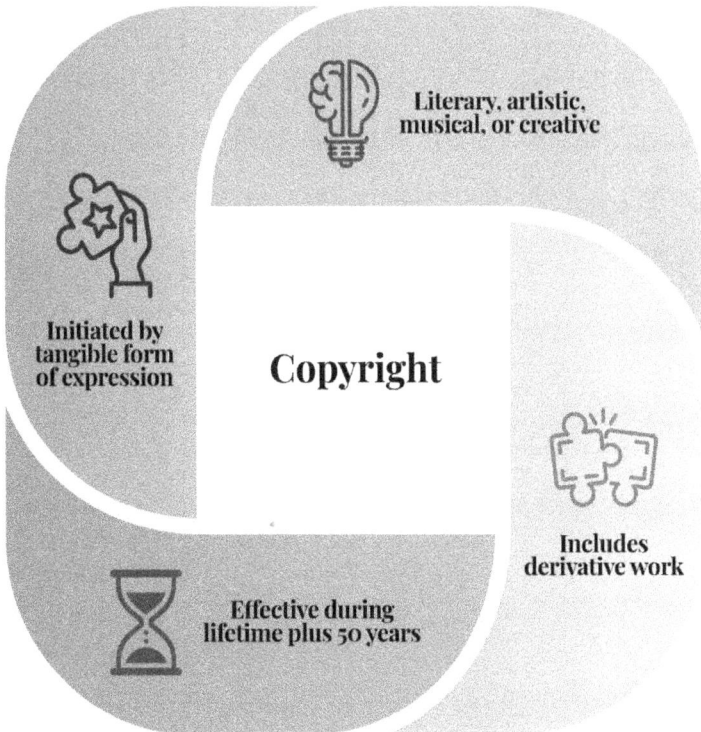

Literary, artistic, musical, or creative

Initiated by tangible form of expression

Copyright

Includes derivative work

Effective during lifetime plus 50 years

Copyrights do not cover the ideas and information themselves; rather they cover the form or manner in which ideas and information are expressed. So, for example, if a particular individual creates a story about a flying car named Spot, the individual car might earn a copyright, but that copyright would not cover all flying cars in other stories by other authors. Others could write stories about flying cars, but those named Spot could be in violation of the copyright. Copyrights are often enforceable during the life of the author and can extend for decades after the author's death, depending on the jurisdiction. In the United States, the work has copyright protection for the lifetime of the creator plus fifty years.

Copyrights will typically not cover names of products, business-es, organizations, or groups, pseudonyms of individuals, titles of works, catchwords, catchphrases, mottoes, slogans, short advertising expressions, and the listings of ingredients in recipes, labels, and formulas. Several of these could be covered under trademark or patent protection.

Reflection Question: Other than in this book, where was the last place you saw a copyright?

One other exception to most intellectual property protection is the con-cept of **fair use**, which includes criticism, commentary, news reporting, teaching, scholarship, or research. Criteria for fair use depends on: (1) the purpose and character of one's use, (2) the nature of the protected work, (3) what amount and proportion of the whole work was taken, and (4) the effect of the use upon the potential market for or value of the protected work. A common exception under fair use is educational purposes, where protected work can be used and presented as part of the learning process. This book uses relevant Seinfeld clips under the fair use provisions so as not to violate the owner's copyright protections.

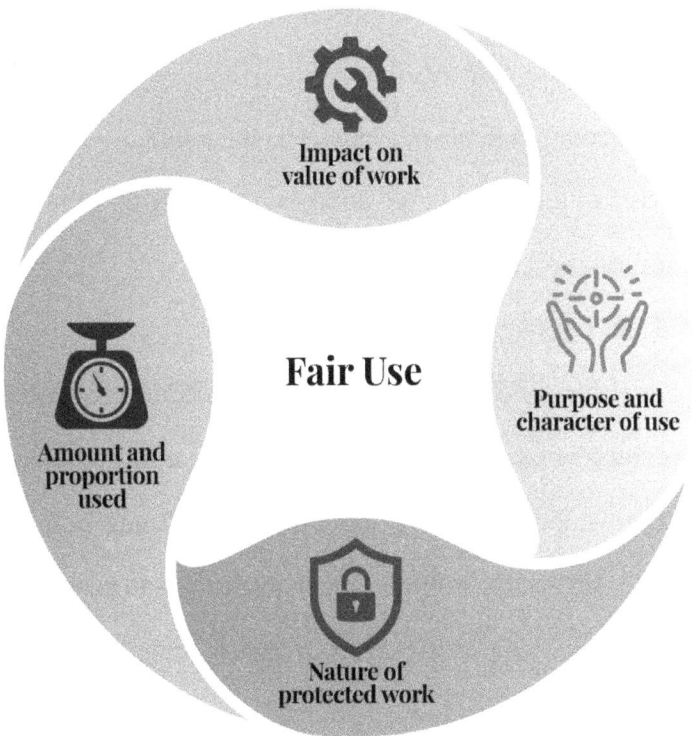

Trade Secrets

Each of the previously mentioned protections of intellectual property require some sort of disclosure in order to be enforced. One other form of protection, **trade secrets**, lies in the action of keeping the production process, formulas, ingredients, designs, patterns, source code of computer programs, and other such proprietary trade practices a secret. A classic example of this is the formula for Coca-Cola® products, which is reportedly kept in a secret vault at the company headquarters; only a handful of select people are said to know the combination. Other trade secrets include customer lists, strategic plans, research and development, pricing information, marketing techniques, and production processes.

The first step to protecting trade secrets is to identify the information used to operate the business that:

- is considered not generally known to the public,
- is a basis of competitive advantage and economic value because the information is not publicly known, and
- motivates efforts to maintain secrecy.

The next step is to create policies and procedures to protect those trade secrets, such as physical barriers to guard the information (safes, passwords, alarms, locks, badges), legal agreements (nondisclosure or noncompete clauses), and a culture of responsibility and accountability. If a firm has taken reasonable measures to protect trade secrets and the information provides economic value to that firm, others that engage in corporate or economic espionage to obtain these trade secrets could be in violation of both federal and state law and prosecuted as such. As long as the secrets are not disclosed to the public, firms may enjoy protection indefinitely.

Trade Secrets

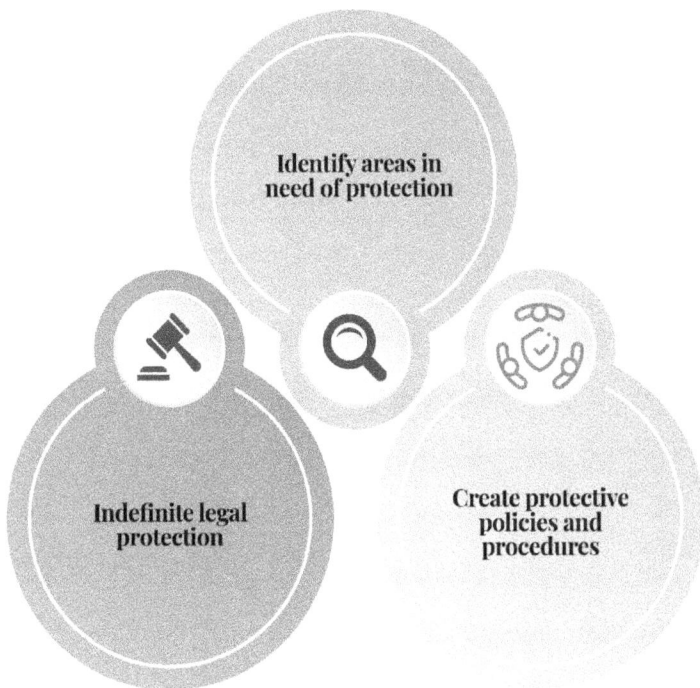

Identify areas in
need of protection

Indefinite legal
protection

Create protective
policies and
procedures

One area of concern in this regard comes when products contain potentially toxic or hazardous materials. Because the ingredients or formulas of these products might be protected as a trade secret to help ensure competitors don't analyze and replicate their chemical composition, they might not be disclosed to the public, who as a result might have an incomplete understanding of the potential harm from using the products in question.

SenSei

Seinfeld Sensei Application

The protection of trade secrets is extremely important in helping to ensure the success of an entrepreneurial enterprise. George showed surprising resilience when safeguarding some valuable information.

Season 7, Episode 7 "The Secret Code" (3:57)

George was unwilling to share his ATM code with anyone and only did so under emergency and life-threatening conditions. Entrepreneurs need to be similarly diligent to protect their trade secrets.

Unfortunately, not everyone in the Seinfeld group was as stalwart as George when it came to protecting proprietary information. Kramer had something valuable but could not keep it hidden.

Season 9, Episode 14 "The Strongbox" (2:47)

Kramer was unable to safeguard the key to his strongbox, and Jerry kept finding it (without even trying very hard). As it turned out, the box wasn't even locked, so if entrepreneurs want to make sure their trade secrets remain secret, they need to do a much better job than Kramer.

Elaine also showed vulnerability when trusted with some important secrets.

Season 9, Episode 8 "The Betrayal" (4:21)

Although Elaine often bragged about her vault, apparently too many people knew that "peach schnapps" was the combination.

Chapter 14: Entrepreneurial Marketing

Big Question Question: What are some cost-effective techniques entrepreneurs can use to market their products and services?

With limited resources, new entrepreneurial ventures need to be creative in planning their marketing strategies. The following are some ways for entrepreneurial firms to make the most out of limited resources.

Bootstrapping

The essence of **bootstrapping** is using available resources to solve problems faced by the firm. This often relies on the ingenuity and creativity of entrepreneurs and their founding teams to do more with less. Endless ways to finance new ideas exist, but marketing a startup with limited resources can be a great way to encourage innovation. A modest budget can encourage entrepreneurs to flex their creative muscles and generate unique ways to share their vision with the world. The following are a few suggestions for how to successfully market a new product or service with limited experience, brand reputation, and financial resources.

1. Always be marketing. Answer questions about what you do with a short description (perhaps using your elevator pitch). So when someone asks, "What do you do for a living?" rather than simply answering, "I'm an entrepreneur" (vague and uninformative) or "I run a small business" (conjures images of a tiny neighborhood store), use this encounter as an opportunity to generate word-of-mouth marketing for the business. Although entrepreneurs who go on and on about their businesses can become tiresome, treating every new meeting as an opportunity to both share information about and to collect data for the entrepreneurial solution is a low-cost way to improve the business.

2. Create a compelling story. Most companies start with an opportunity recognized and an alert entrepreneur who acts to capitalize on that opportunity. Instead of telling a boring, ordinary story, entrepreneurs should develop a narrative that differentiates their company from others and sparks conversation. If their startup supports a certain cause, entrepreneurs should emphasize this in their stories. If the business idea was the result of some troubling life event, mentioning it may inspire others and can be memorable.

3. Include others in the story. When discussing the business with others, asking them questions about problems they face is not only a great way to help them feel important but can also be a valuable tool in understanding how others might be dealing with the problem the entrepreneur is trying to solve. Such questions help others feel connected to the business and allow entrepreneurs to obtain data from a potential customer.

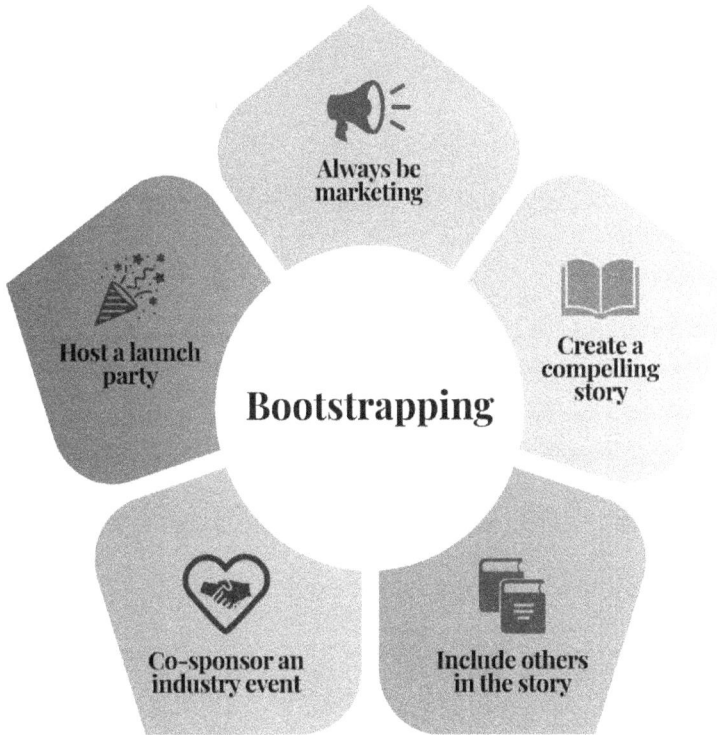

4. Co-sponsor an industry event. Most industries sponsor trade shows, conferences, award shows, and so forth for organization members. Planners often seek out sponsors to help organize and fund such events, which provides entrepreneurs with a fantastic niche marketing opportunity. When entrepreneurs consider attending such an industry event, exploring if any sponsorship spots are open can be promising. Or, even better, entrepreneurs can spotlight their startup to further engage attendees. Aside from giving the entrepreneurial firm some publicity, co-sponsoring an event can allow entrepreneurs to engage and network with their target demographic and to learn more about important industry players.

5. Host an inexpensive launch party. Whenever a new product or service is being released, making a public event out of it can be an exciting way to market the startup and to get people to experiment with it. For example, if the entrepreneurial idea comes with an app, getting people to download and use the app is of paramount importance. For the price of pizzas, some T-shirts, Frisbees, bumper stickers, or other inexpensive marketing materials, a sponsored launch party can provide access to customers and teach them about the attributes of the product or service. Admission to the party can be a download of the app, a test of the product, or an email address for promotions and other information, giving potential customers exposure to the app or product and helping increase adoption.

Reflection Question: Which of the above bootstrapping techniques have you seen prove successful for marketing new startups?

Social Media

Technology is constantly changing and is also changing the way people interact with each other, including how entrepreneurs interact with potential customers. One positive outcome of social media like Facebook, Instagram, and Twitter is how accessible people are and how willing they are to share their likes, dislikes, and other preferences. Entrepreneurs with limited resources can target their message to those who have expressed an interest, which increases the efficiency of marketing dollars spent.

1. Don't just sell—engage. When it comes to social media, engaging their target demographic without looking like they're just trying to advertise is easy for entrepreneurs. Paying attention to activity related to the venture idea can create connections and be a subtle entrance to marketing. For example, restaurant ventures might leave encouraging comments on photos of people's food, sports equipment retailers might repost articles on a local high school team's recent win, travel websites might comment on recent vacation photos, and so forth. Entrepreneurs can build trust and loyalty by showing support of their local community and their growing online following.

2. Carve a niche and build industry credibility. Creating a blog, newsletter, podcast, or informational post to offer an insider's perspective is a great way to build a culture around a brand. Hosting a webinar or podcast can help viewers and listeners learn more about important issues in the industry's and market segment's space. Networking and sharing expertise with others can encourage potential customers to learn more about an entrepreneur's industry and serve as a platform to demonstrate the entrepreneur's abilities to an interested community. This not only helps establish the entrepreneur as an expert but also increases brand awareness when the time for a purchasing decision comes around.

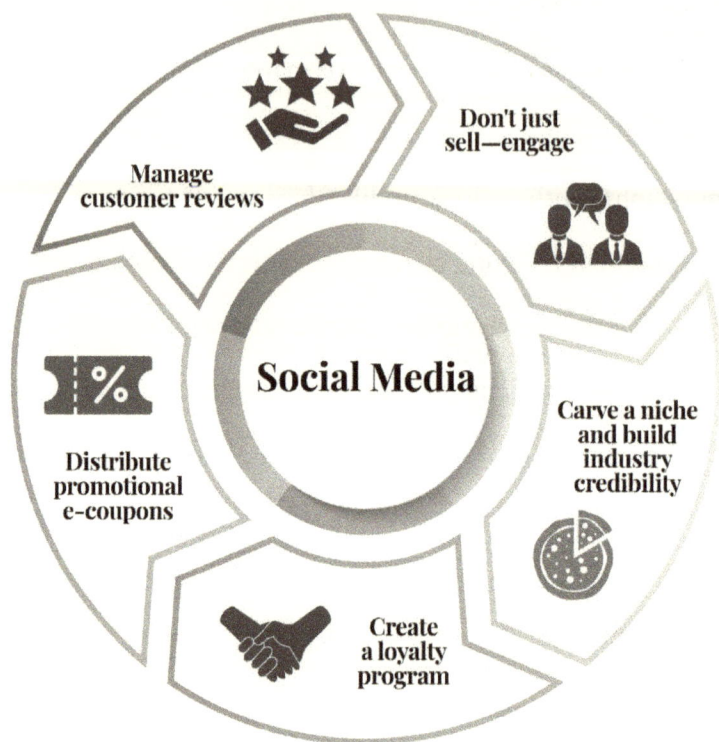

Social Media

Manage customer reviews

Don't just sell—engage

Carve a niche and build industry credibility

Create a loyalty program

Distribute promotional e-coupons

3. Create a loyalty program. Customer acquisition costs are often the highest marketing expenses for new ventures, so keeping existing customers should be a high priority. Enrolling customers in a loyalty program, through which they can earn free or discounted products or services based on continued patronage, reduces the need to continually rely on getting new customers for more revenues and solidifies a strong repeat customer base to assist with word-of-mouth marketing. Sometimes a network of ventures, in which several local businesses band together to offer rewards based on patronage of any of the partners' locations, can be used to increase the attractiveness of a loyalty program. For example, a bakery could partner with a nearby hot beverage store where a purchase at one business qualifies the customer for a 10 percent discount at the other. Linking the loyalty program to customers' existing social media accounts (e.g., providing coupons for mentions or likes on Facebook, Instagram, Twitter, and so forth) can also be an effective way to find new customers while rewarding existing ones.

4. Distribute promotional e-coupons. Utilizing email and social media marketing to distribute coupons is a great way to reach current and potential customers for a relatively low cost. Those who have already invested in the venture's products or services will appreciate being thanked for their business, and people who have yet to make a purchase might be more incentivized to try out something new. Coupons also don't technically cost the venture anything until they're redeemed and utilizing "buy one get one free" promotions can guarantee revenues upon which the company can build.

5. Manage customer reviews. Online reviews can make or break a firm. If customers post rave reviews online, new users will be much more likely to give a young entrepreneurial firm a try. A negative review (or a slew of negative reviews) can derail all the entrepreneur's efforts and can quickly impede the path to success. Alert entrepreneurs should monitor their various social media outlets and respond to both positive and negative reviews. A simple thank you to customers posting positive reviews can endear them to the new firm. An honest and open response with a promise to work to fix the problem identified in a negative review can help turn one star into more and can demonstrate to existing and potential customers that the entrepreneur cares about those customers. One area of caution is trying to influence customers' reviews; companies that try to suppress or pressure users to change their negative reviews could face a public relations backlash, resulting in a loss of public trust and a damaged reputation.

Reflection Question: Think of a recent social media interaction from a business you patronize. What was particularly effective about their social media activities? What could have been improved?

Seinfeld Sensei Application

Jerry needed a haircut for an event hosted by Elaine but ran into some trouble when he attempted to get a fresh look.

Season 5, Episode 8 "The Barber" (2:43)

The reviews for Enzo Manganero were predominantly negative, which hurt his ability to gain new or to retain existing clients. Gino, on the other hand, had rave reviews and many satisfied customers, including Kramer. Although Jerry felt bad for Enzo and didn't want to hurt his feelings, his haircutting needs were ultimately not being satisfied. Entrepreneurs can greatly benefit from positive word of mouth but need to avoid negative customer reviews as much as possible.

Advocates

Instead of relying solely on the voice of the firm or its employees, sometimes entrepreneurial firms can leverage others outside the company to assist with marketing. **Advocates** (sometimes called evangelists) are influential people who can generate positive publicity for the firm, often in exchange for free or discounted products or services, further helping resource-constrained entrepreneurs effectively communicate the value they have to offer.

1. Scratch their back, they'll scratch yours. Since entrepreneurs may find difficulty introducing their young firms to the public, one effective way to create a following and generate word-of-mouth interest is to provide samples and giveaways, and through promotions. For example, one effective marketing action is to reach out to eager members of the target audience and offer up all or part of the venture's product or service in return for likes, a review, and shares on social media. Those who participate get a cool new item or experience to share with their friends, while the venture gets legitimacy and visibility, creating a mutually beneficial outcome. Young firms don't want to give up their entire stock all at once, but sharing it with a select few influential advocates could give a new venture a marketing advantage. Including other firms that sell complementary products in a win-win marketing partnership can also be a cost-effective way to increase brand awareness.

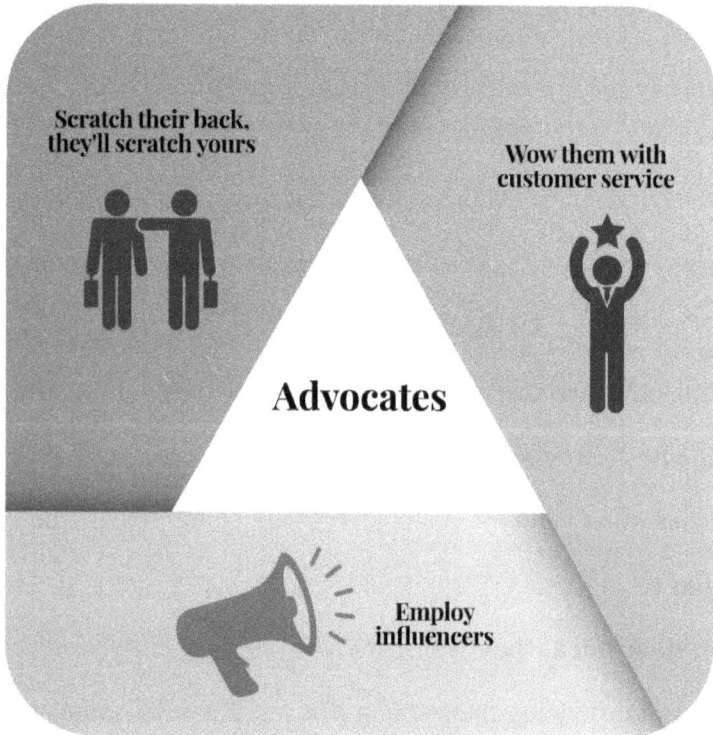

2. Employ influencers. As the firm identifies a specific demographic as its target audience, utilizing someone who exemplifies that audience to help market and sell a product or service can be very effective. For example, having outgoing, stereotypical college students market to other, similar college students can be more effective than utilizing employees who don't fit that description. Oftentimes these influencers can be interns or part-time employees who are more cost effective than full-time paid spokespeople or high-cost celebrities.

3. Wow them with customer service. Although customer service alone is rarely enough to create a sustainable competitive advantage, going above and beyond to ensure customers have a phenomenal first experience can go a long way to making sure those customers have repeated experiences with products and services. Showing how much the customer's patronage is valued and appreciated can create a lasting bond, and the positive word of mouth generated by these memorable experiences can turn a loyal customer into a great marketing outlet to other potential customers.

Seinfeld Sensei Application

In this example, Jerry had an opportunity to serve as a celebrity influencer, helping a woman in fashion increase sales and bring more notoriety to her innovative new designs.

Season 5, Episode 2 "The Puffy Shirt" (4:56)

Although Jerry's agreeing to wear the puffy shirt on TV led to initial success, his later bad mouthing of it led to the demise of Kramer's girlfriend's career. So even though celebrity endorsements can be a great marketing win for an entrepreneur, a much more effective strategy comes when the celebrity actually knows what he or she is endorsing.

Promotions are another way to entice customers to try an entrepreneur's product or service while maintaining lower degrees of risk and uncertainty

.

Season 7, Episode 22 "The Invitations" (3:13)

Kramer tries to cash in on a bank's promotional offer of one hundred dollars if one of its tellers fails to say hello. Is "hey" the same as "hello"? Apparently it's close enough for both the bank and for Kramer.

Chapter 15: Founding Team

Big Question Question: What are important components to consider when forming a founding team?

Founding Team Characteristics

Leaders of organizations play an integral role in the creation, development, and ultimate success of that organization. Particularly for new or young entrepreneurial firms, the leader's characteristics, goals, objectives, ethics, morals, strategies, and decisions shape how a firm conducts its activities. Often these are imprinted in a firm's DNA and become the foundation of future activities for years or even decades to come. As such, founders have an important responsibility to make sure the formation of a new firm is done with this in mind.

Rarely does an individual entrepreneur possess all the skills, abilities, and competencies necessary to create and grow a thriving enterprise, so a team is usually more effective in achieving success. This drives the importance of a team-based environment, where other team members can help compensate for the areas in which the entrepreneur might not possess the necessary qualities or expertise to be successful. As such, individual founders often assemble a **founding team** to help bring their idea into reality and to enhance its profitability potential.

An old adage of entrepreneurship advises that "an A team with a B idea is better than a B team with an A idea."

Reflection question: Why is an A team with a B idea better than a B team with an A idea?

Ideas often change and evolve as new information is attained, and the right set of skills is often needed to be able to adapt to those changes. The key is to have the right people on the team who can grow and implement the idea as it changes rather than remain stuck to an old idea. At the end of the day, execution is often just as important as the idea itself, so the right team can execute any idea, whereas the wrong team can destroy a great idea.

Whom should entrepreneurs choose for their founding team? Most traditional hiring is based on the functional needs of the business. For example, if the founders have an accounting background, they might want to hire someone who has an expertise and experience in marketing to balance out the team's skills. Or if the product or service has a high level of technical requirements, hiring someone who can understand and implement the technology is important. For entrepreneurial firms, however, technical skills are usually not enough. Due to the highly uncertain and fluctuating nature of most entrepreneurial environments, founding team members need to be able to thrive in such a situation. Whereas existing organizations might have established norms, clear job descriptions, and a highly structured work environment, entrepreneurial firms are usually making things up as they go, so founding team members need to be able to contribute to this evolution. When this creative and entrepreneurial behavior can be harnessed among a group of founders with differing skills and perspectives, extraordinary things can be achieved.

Some people are comfortable with ideas that challenge existing norms and capitalize on entrepreneurial opportunities, whereas others prefer smaller increments of change, such as ideas about how to improve the jobs they currently do or their existing working environment in less radical ways. The latter might not be the best fit for new entrepreneurial firms. So even though expertise, competence, and knowledge base are necessary aspects of any top management team member, those alone are usually not sufficient in a highly entrepreneurial environment. Often some sort of entrepreneurial orientation or mindset is also needed, which can allow team members to thrive in uncertain and less structured situations. Early members of the organization might be asked to take on more than one role until someone else is hired to fill the spot, so being able to learn on the go might be important. Some other important entrepreneurial characteristics include openness to experience, tolerance of ambiguity, internal locus of control (being self-directed), curiosity, risk taking, adaptability, and flexibility. Having a founding team with technical expertise and competence combined with an entrepreneurial spirit can be a winning formula for early success.

Founding Team Characteristics

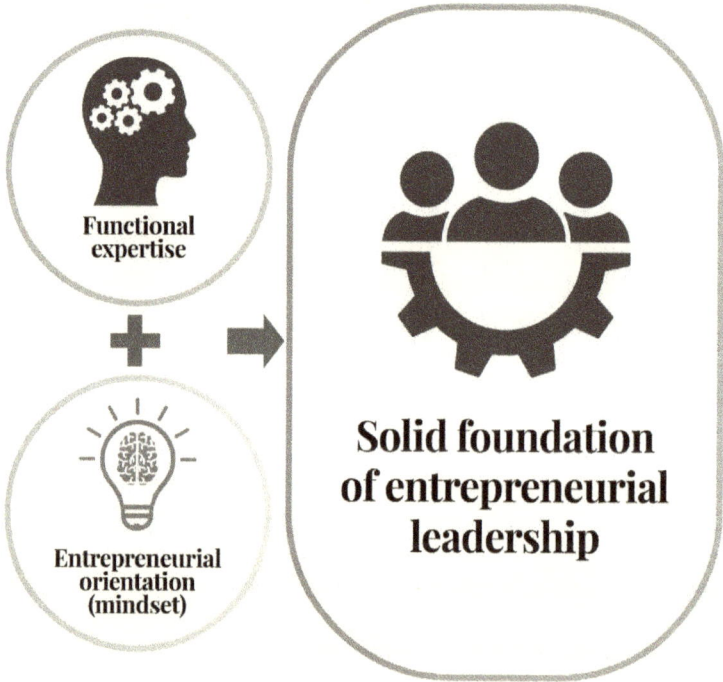

Seinfeld Sensei Application

George faced a particular problem when attempting to solidify his legacy and reached out to others for help.

George realized he didn't have the expertise and resources necessary to move the Frogger machine, so he created a team, with Kramer providing the tape, Slippery Pete rigging the wiring, and Shlomo driving the truck. But the team had a hard time capturing the vision of his endeavor, so even though they were more or less competent in their areas of expertise, their lack of entrepreneurial vision and problem-solving abilities hindered the project. Entrepreneurs must consider both the technical skills and entrepreneurial orientation of their early employees to ensure their goals and objectives are accomplished.

Division of Equity

One of the biggest challenges when starting a business is deciding how the equity of the new firm will be split among the founding team. Although many books and techniques have been suggested for how to do this, no one way exists for doing it properly. Nonetheless, creating a **founders' agreement** is an extremely valuable way to address critical aspects of the business.

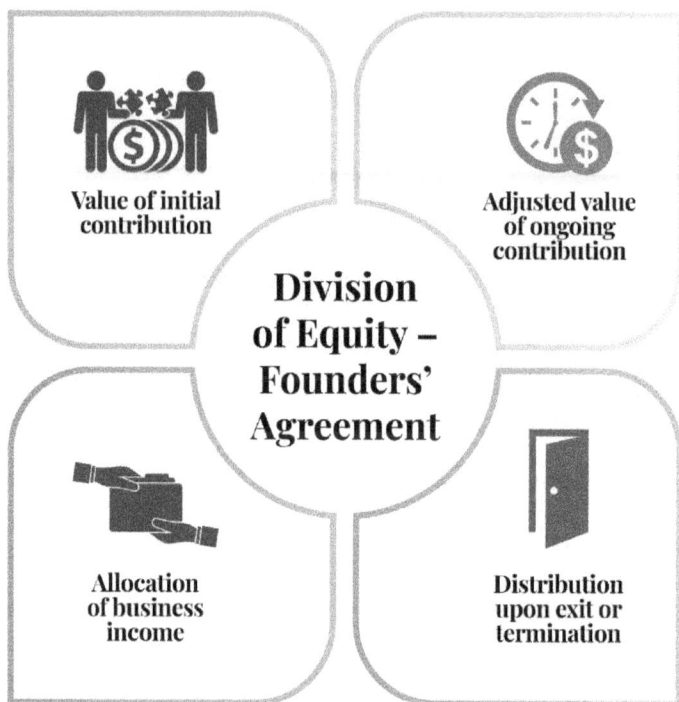

Value of initial contribution

Adjusted value of ongoing contribution

Division of Equity – Founders' Agreement

Allocation of business income

Distribution upon exit or termination

Typically, when creating an agreement, the first step is to determine who is bringing what to the business. For example, does one founder own any intellectual property, such as a patent for the idea or product from which the business was started? Is one founder contributing more cash or property to the new business than others? Other notable contributions from founders include time, relationships, credit/loans, facilities, supplies, equipment, and other machinery. To the extent possible, objective, third-party measurements—such as fair market value—should be used to determine the value the input of each founding member. The main point of the agreement is to reduce conflict and emotional interference when big events inevitably occur as the business evolves. Founders need to have the tough conversations around issues such as the value of each member's initial contribution, how that might change over time, how business income is going to be distributed on an annual basis, and how the equity in the business is going to be distributed upon exit or termination.

Seinfeld Sensei Application

George encountered two situations where a clear understanding of the relationships would have been very useful.

Season 9, Episode 14 "The Strongbox" (4:57)

These two situations demonstrate why a clear relationship agreement is so important. George couldn't effectively dissolve his current relationship, and he couldn't agree to terms with his new relationship. When entrepreneurs are going into business—especially with close friends or family members—having those difficult conversations upfront helps to minimize the likelihood of the relationship being damaged down the road.

Jerry also had some issues with blurry relationship boundaries. What started out one way quickly transformed into something much less sophisticated.

Season 9, Episode 19 "The Maid" (4:48)

Even though Jerry initially had an appropriate employer-employee relationship with his maid, they failed to adhere to the established guidelines for that relationship to remain harmonious. Setting clear expectations for employment responsibilities, including termination procedures, can help reduce or remove misunderstandings and awkward situations, particularly when both personal and professional relationships are involved. Founders' agreements and other formal employee contracts are tools entrepreneurs can use to ensure relationships are managed and boundaries are clearly defined.

Chapter 16: Entrepreneurial Advice Networks

Big Question Question: What advice networks are available for entrepreneurs to help create and grow their new ventures?

As entrepreneurs work through their business ideas and begin to form new ventures, various advice and support networks exist to help. Depending on the stage, rate of growth, goals, objectives, etc. of the venture, various options exist to help the entrepreneur become successful.

Reflection Question: If you were to create a startup, what are some sources of advice you would utilize?

Incubators

Some aspiring entrepreneurs, recognizing the opportunity to help other aspiring entrepreneurs, have created organizations to assist new ventures in their development. These **incubators** provide valuable services to help entrepreneurs get through the initial hurdles of starting a new enterprise. Incubators usually have an application process, and acceptance criteria vary from program to program, but typically only those with promising business ideas and feasible business plans are accepted. Incubators often provide working space with computing services and shared administrative functions, funding for market research and prototype development, legal and accounting services, and other **key resources** for growing a new venture. Perhaps most importantly, incubators provide mentoring, feedback, and guidance to help navigate through the challenging process of creating and growing an entrepreneurial enterprise. Incubators provide opportunities to network with key stakeholders, including possible strategic partners and funding sources. **Graduation** from the incubator usually depends on the entrepreneurial firm achieving certain milestones, which are agreed upon by both parties. Many incubators are supported by government entities or other **economic development organizations** but will still charge **fees**. Some of these fees come in the form of an equity stake in the entrepreneurial firm, but these stakes can vary greatly based on the services offered and time spent in the incubator.

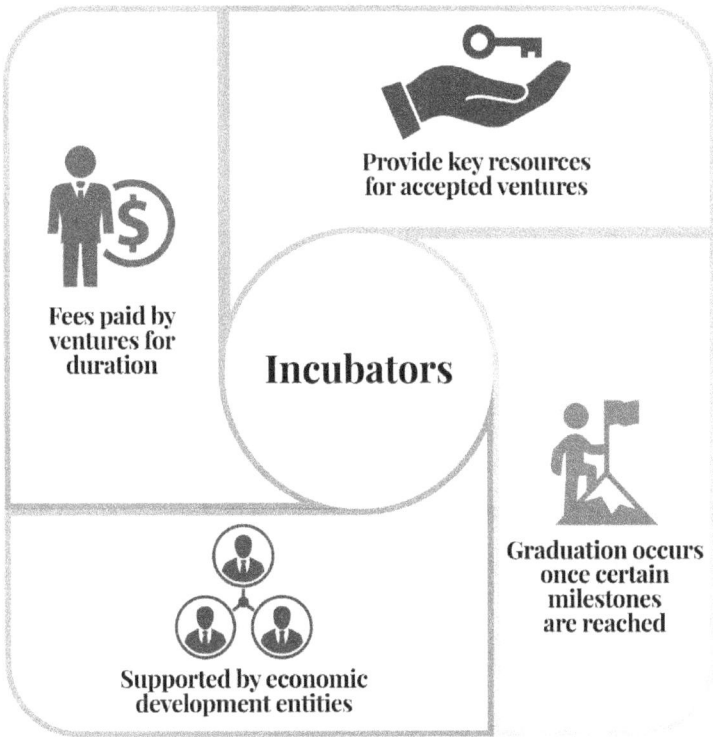

Incubators

- Fees paid by ventures for duration
- Provide key resources for accepted ventures
- Supported by economic development entities
- Graduation occurs once certain milestones are reached

Accelerators

Another variation of the formalized advice network is the **accelerator**, which takes more developed entrepreneurial firms and advances them to commercialization of their business ideas. Although similar to incubators in that they provide working space, funding, networking, and mentorship, most accelerators are privately funded and expect a more significant equity stake in the venture in exchange for the services provided. Some other key qualities of accelerators that distinguish them from incubators include:

- a seed investment made in the startup in exchange for some equity ownership,

- the focus on small teams rather than an individual founder,

- the "cohort" model of those accepted, wherein firms start and end together to provide feedback and support (and competition!) to other teams in the cohort, and

- the finite nature of the accelerator (often three to six months).

Accelerators

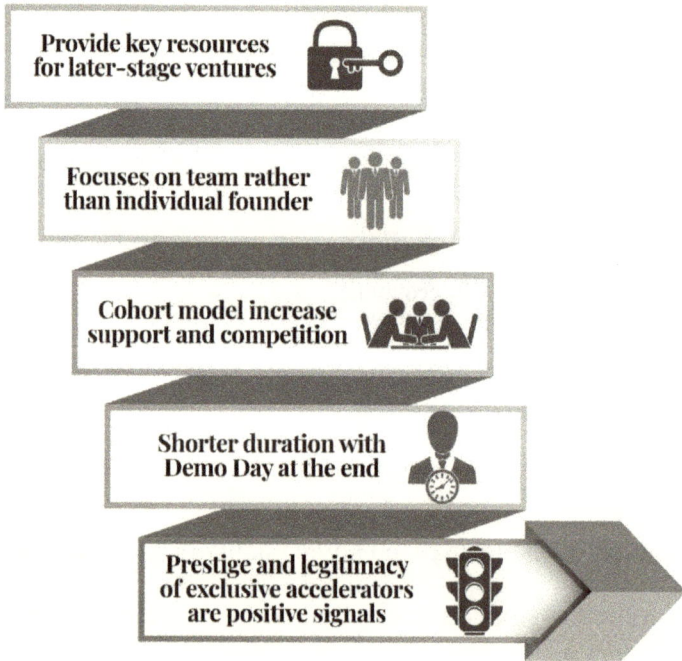

Provide key resources
for later-stage ventures

Focuses on team rather
than individual founder

Cohort model increase
support and competition

Shorter duration with
Demo Day at the end

Prestige and legitimacy
of exclusive accelerators
are positive signals

Most accelerators culminate in a "Demo Day" where the firms in the cohort present their ideas to potential investors and other strategic partners for the opportunity to win money and to be invested in by angels or venture capitalists. Startups accepted into some of the more well-known accelerators (such as Y Combinator and TechStars) can also benefit from the prestige of being selected, which is often a signal to the marketplace the firm has a high degree of investment potential.

Universities

Institutions of higher education have also been highly supportive of entrepreneurial activity. Most major **universities** have technology transfer or technology licensing offices to oversee inventions created by professors and other employees. The purpose of most of these offices is to assist with and to oversee the process of bringing research developments to market, since most individuals engaged in university research are not experienced entrepreneurs. In exchange, universities often retain the intellectual property of the invention and typically split ownership of and receive royalties on sales of the commercialized product. These royalties help reimburse the university for the resources used by the inventor and are used to fund future research. Although universities are not founded with the purpose of creating new and innovative products and services, leveraging the entrepreneurial activities of their professors and employees can add value to society and can also reward inventors for their discoveries. Universities also offer support to students in the form of classes, clubs, mentorship, pitch and plan competitions, guest speakers, and other resources to help entrepreneurs discover and develop their entrepreneurial ideas. Although most universities require at least one member of the founding team to be a student at that university, entrepreneurial ventures with these connections benefit greatly from the various resources universities can offer.

Universities

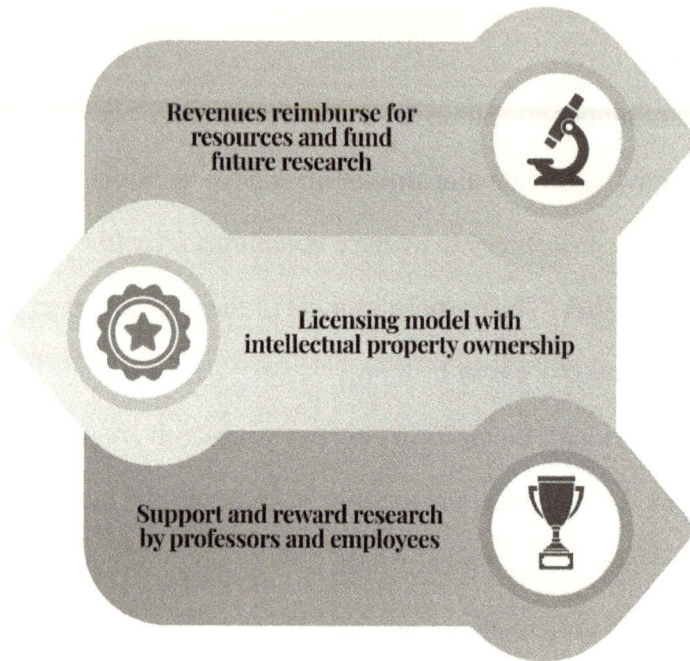

Revenues reimburse for resources and fund future research

Licensing model with intellectual property ownership

Support and reward research by professors and employees

A famous example of university-supported innovation is that of Gatorade. In the 1960s, research scientists at the University of Florida (home of the Gators) were looking for a way to help their student athletes replace electrolytes and other fluids lost during physical activity. What they created helped their sports programs to be more successful, and they decided to seize this potential entrepreneurial opportunity by creating a product for the general public. Thus, Gatorade was born, and the result of the partnership between researchers and the university has been a highly successful business.

Seinfeld Sensei Application

Entrepreneurs need to choose the source of advice that works best for them given their goals, resources, and opportunities. George missed out on some great opportunities because he chose the wrong person from whom to solicit advice.

Season 3, Episode 15 "The Suicide" (4:25)

George went to a psychic instead of a more legitimate source to get some guidance, and Kramer benefited. Great advice exists if entrepreneurs know where to look for it, and choosing a source appropriate for the entrepreneurs' situations can go a long way to helping them receive critical resources for success.

Chapter 17: Social Entrepreneurship

Big Question Question: What motivations and opportunities exist for businesses other than profits?

Although all ventures should be started in order to solve an important problem, some motives beyond simply making a profit are relevant. Entrepreneurs can start businesses for various reasons, including to benefit underrepresented populations, the environment, or other groups or causes in which the founders believe. This is called **social entrepreneurship**, defined as activities and processes undertaken to enhance social wealth, which can also include helping the environment (also known as "ecopreneurship").

Reflection Question: How is the social entrepreneurship process different than other entrepreneurial pursuits?

Social Entrepreneurship Process

The **social entrepreneurship process** involves recognizing a perceived social opportunity, translating that social opportunity into a business concept, and identifying and acquiring the necessary resources to execute the startup's goals.

By and large the exact same sound business principles necessary to make a successful entrepreneurial enterprise should be followed in the case of a socially conscious venture. Yet unique challenges for social entrepreneurship include balancing competing interests and getting people to believe the business really is concerned about its underlying cause. A phenomenon called "green washing" exists to describe a business pretending to be interested in solving an environmental problem when it is really only concerned with making money. One potential red flag is when the following phrase is used: "A portion of the proceeds will be donated to. . ." This ambiguity of how much the cause is benefitting could raise suspicion and might call into question the true motives of the entrepreneurial venture. The question often comes down to a means versus ends argument. If the business is created as a means to solve an important social or environmental problem, the motives of the entrepreneur are more likely to be pure; but if the social or environmental cause is being used as a means of making profit, the sincerity of the entrepreneur could be called into question.

In addition, a constant struggle exists between finding a balance of for-profit considerations and achieving the social or environmental purpose of the entrepreneurial firm. For example, if entrepreneurs want to help underprivileged people, they could just give away the product or service for free, but this would not be a sustainable business model. If the firm is unprofitable, it will not be around to help solve the problem for which it was created in the first place. On the other hand, if it is only concerned with making a profit, it will be no different than any other for-profit organization (and may even be considered worse). Entrepreneurs who are transparent and align their business activities with a focus on the same social cause they are trying to help can often convince others they are sincere and legitimate.

Reflection Question: Can you think of social entrepreneurship ventures whose motives are questionable? What makes you think this? Conversely, can you think of socially conscious startups that seem sincere and legitimate? What actions by the founders of these startups help you feel this way?

Triple Bottom Line (Three Ps)

The impact of social entrepreneurship is usually captured by Triple Bottom Line measures, which highlight the purpose of the venture beyond simple profitability. These measures are also referred to as the "Three Ps":

- Social performance (**People**) is made up of unemployment rate, median household income, relative poverty, percentage of population with a postsecondary degree or certificate, average commute time, violent crimes per capita, or health-adjusted life expectancy.

- Environmental performance (**Planet**) includes hazardous chemical concentrations, selected priority pollutants, electricity consumption, fossil fuel consumption, solid waste management, hazardous waste management, or change in land use/land cover.
- Economic performance (**Profit**) consists of personal income, cost of underemployment, establishment sizes, job growth, employment distribution by sector, percentage of firms in each sector, or revenue by sector contributing to gross state product.

Triple Bottom Line

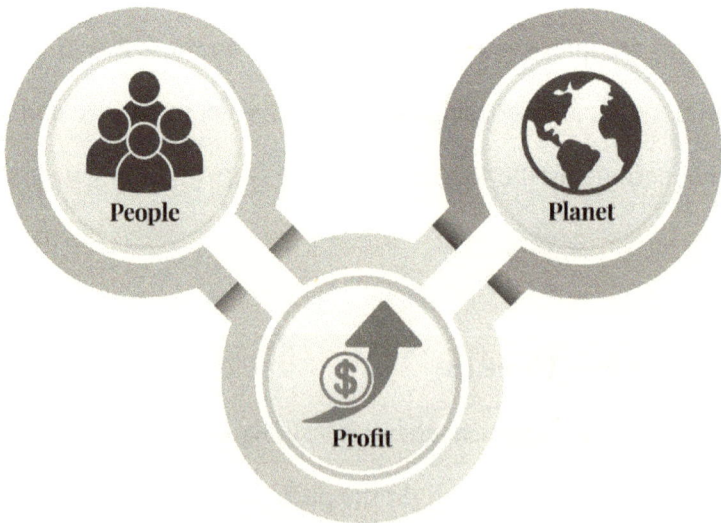

The better entrepreneurs are able to capture and communicate areas in which they are creating and adding value above and beyond simple profit motives, the better their social message will be received by interested stakeholders.

Seinfeld Sensei Application

Kramer recognized a problem and came up with an idea with an environmental purpose, which went beyond simply making a profitable business.

Season 9, Episode 2 "The Voice" (4:46)

Kramer's idea of a bladder for oil tankers could satisfy both for-profit and environmental objectives. Kramer did a good job applying lean entrepreneurship principles by assessing his idea before wasting valuable time, effort, energy, and money chasing after something that wouldn't work. But even though he had lofty and altruistic intentions, his bubble was ultimately burst.

Chapter 18: International Entrepreneurship

Big Question Question: How can entrepreneurs benefit from an international perspective when engaging in entrepreneurial activities?

Reasons for Going International

Often entrepreneurial opportunities exist in other countries or geographic locations. Traditionally, firms have extended their business activities across borders for three main reasons: to increase the market size or demand for their products, to increase economies of scale and learning curve advantages, and to attain location advantages such as access to specialized resources, lower cost labor and other inputs, or convenience to other geographic locations.

Reflection Question: Beyond the reasons stated above, how might startups especially benefit from having an international perspective?

For entrepreneurial firms in particular, sometimes products or services might be better suited to a developing or foreign environment due to regulatory restrictions, competitive saturation, market demand, or the growth stage of the firm. For products or services still in early stages of development, entrepreneurs could experiment with and test out their products in a lower cost, lower risk, or more suitable environment by locating their venture in another country. Entrepreneurs could also learn from the foreign environment to improve the product or service, making it more attractive to and accepted in the home country. Once the potential of the product or service is more established, they could then bring it back to the home country.

Entrepreneurial Reasons for Internationalization

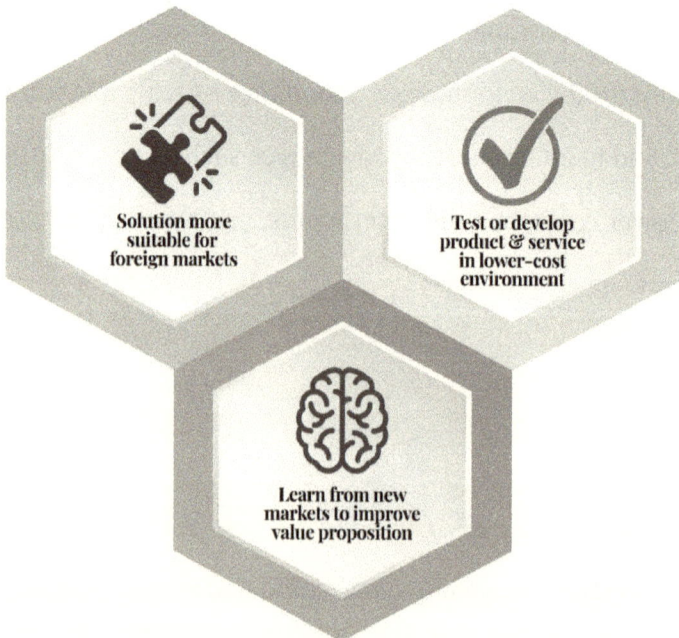

Solution more suitable for foreign markets

Test or develop product & service in lower-cost environment

Learn from new markets to improve value proposition

Seinfeld Sensei Application

George learned from first-hand experience how other countries may be more advanced in finding solutions to important problems.

Season 3, Episode 8 "The Tape" (4:51)

George's praise of a baldness cure from China demonstrated how sometimes problems faced in one country have already been solved in another country, and an alert entrepreneur who is willing to act can capitalize on this asymmetric information to pursue an opportunity in the home country.

In addition, Jerry learned a hard lesson while discovering more about the conditions that existed for his relatives before immigrating to the United States.

Season 2, Episode 2 "The Pony Remark" (4:42)

All too often, entrepreneurs are ethnocentric, believing their country is the best and is vastly superior in every way. Although patriotism is certainly a wonderful thing, entrepreneurs also need to recognize the benefits and advantages people in other countries might enjoy. By having an open mind and willingness to learn from other countries, entrepreneurs can identify and explore new opportunities. Jerry's initial ignorance led him to overlook the value of the pony, which could make useful and valuable contributions to potential customers. Thankfully, Jerry finally realized some benefits of the pony and even hypothesized some interesting applications for it, which could form the basis of an entrepreneurial endeavor.

Chapter 19: Criminal Entrepreneurship

Big Question Question: What happens when solutions to the market's problems are illegal? How do entrepreneurs navigate a realm of blurry legal parameters?

Entrepreneurship deals with a great amount of uncertainty. Most of that uncertainty relates to new ideas and market acceptance, but this chapter uncovers other levels of uncertainty that can exist in industries that face various degrees of legality.

Battle for Legitimacy

The early stages of an industry are often considered an "experiment," where the rules of the game are still being established. This area of extreme uncertainty is one in which a number of entrepreneurial opportunities exist. Entrepreneurship drives the direction of the experiment, and particularly creative and resourceful entrepreneurs can help shape the industry in their favor. At any point, however, due to the questions surrounding the legality of the industry, things could come crashing down. Examples of "criminal" industries include or have included alcohol, tobacco, prostitution, gambling, and numerous types of drugs. These industries have evolved and gone through various stages of uncertainty.

Proponents of regulating these industries have typically argued that these can be a good source of tax revenue, the costs of enforcement will decrease, research will make them safer, and, since demand will exist no matter what, regulation is a better model than the illegal black market.

Reflection Question: Beyond the uncertainty of market demand (whether or not customers will pay for it), what additional sources of uncertainty can exist in illegal or semi legal industries?

One modern example of an industry with blurry legal lines is the cannabis industry, which is still illegal at the federal level and thus introduces additional sources of uncertainty—institutional uncertainty (including banking, regulation, and federal/state disagreements) and additional market uncertainty (customer characteristics, black market, and public perception) among them. These lie beyond the typical sources of uncertainty, such as market demand, technological competence, profitable business models, and a match among the characteristics of the founding team.

Additional Uncertainty

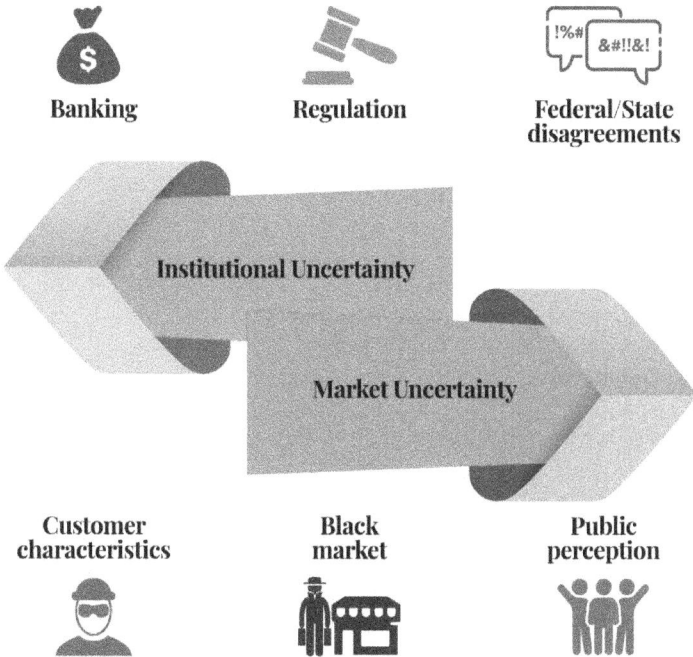

An interesting aspect of some of these industries concerns the reason entrepreneurs enter them in the first place. In the cannabis industry, "purists" who see legalization as an issue of social justice, freedom of expression, and medical necessity see themselves as part of an important social movement. Others, however, primarily see the growth and profit potential of the emerging industry and enter to make money. Sometimes these groups clash, even though the adoption and expansion of the industry should be an interest they have in common. Case in point, in Ohio in 2015, the issue of legalization of cannabis for medical and recreational purposes was put on the ballot for voters to decide. But the bill was worded in such a way that only a small group of businesses would be able to control the growing, distribution, and sale of the product, thereby creating a de facto oligopoly. At this point, purist organizations that would normally be in favor of the legalization of cannabis spoke out and campaigned against the bill because they would have rather seen it remain illegal than have seen it legalized under these restrictive and business-minded conditions. These clashing identities and purposes can be an interesting dynamic not always seen in other types of industries.

Seinfeld Sensei Application

Numerous members of the *Seinfeld* cast were presented with a particular domestic equipment issue and explored some "black market" solutions to their problems.

Season 7, Episode 16 "The Shower Head" (3:55)

Going to the black market forced Kramer and Newman to deal with a somewhat suspect business partner, and the uncertainty of how the product would even work was tougher to deal with in an illegal world.

Jerry and his friends were also brought into a seedy world that sought to bring cutting edge films to the masses in a less than legitimate manner.

Season 8, Episode 4 "The Little Kicks" (4:37)

Jerry and George faced the added risks and uncertainties of operating in an illegal world. Brody had created a nice side business bringing bootlegged versions of theater films to the streets and forced Jerry, who showed particular potential with his skills, into this illegal activity. George, looking to impress a woman as the "bad boy," willingly participated in the bootlegging but paid the price when he was caught. Both experienced the additional uncertainty – and downside – of working outside the law, which should be avoided by entrepreneurs who are interested in creating sustainable, legitimate business enterprises.

References

Covey, Stephen. *The 8th Habit: From Effectiveness to Greatness*. New York: Free Press, 2006.

Kander, Diana. *All In Startup: Launching a New Idea When Everything Is on the Line*. Hoboken, NJ: John Wiley & Sons, Inc., 2014.

Kuratko, Donald. *Entrepreneurship: Theory, Process, Practice*. 9th ed. Boston: Cengage Learning, 2013.

Osterwalder, Alexander and Yves Pignuer. *Business Model Generation: A Handbook for Visionaries, Game Changers, and Challengers*. Hoboken, NJ: John Wiley & Sons, Inc., 2010.

Ries, Eric. *The Lean Startup: How Today's Entrepreneurs Use Continuous Innovation to Create Radically Successful Businesses*. New York: Crown, 2001.

Silverstein, Jack. "UT Business Prof Shares 5 Tips for Giving Great Presentations." Built in ATX. October 23, 2017.

Toren, Matthew. "7 Creative Strategies for Marketing Your Startup on a Tight Budget." Entrepreneur.com article 277343, June 16, 2016.

Zacharakis, Andrew, Stephen Spinelli, and Jeffrey A. Timmons. *Business Plans that Work: A Guide for Small Business*. 2nd Edition. New York, NY: McGraw Hill, 2011.

Quick Episode Reference Guide

Chapter 1. Entrepreneurial Process

Season 6, Episode 17 "The Doorman" (4:08)

Chapter 2. Becoming an Entrepreneur

Season 2, Episode 7 "The Revenge" (3:33)

Chapter 3. Entrepreneurial Characteristics

Season 7, Episode 18 "The Friar's Club" (4:52)

Season 6, Episode 17 "The Jimmy" (3:40)

Season 5, Episode 6 "The Lip Reader" (4:07)

Season 7, Episode 6 "The Soup Nazi" (1:59)

Season 7, Episode 20 "The Bottle Deposit" (3:56)

Chapter 4. Personal Entrepreneurial Risks

Season 8, Episode 3 "The Bizarro Jerry" (4:31)

Season 1, Episode 5 "The Stock Tip" (3:42)

Chapter 5. Entrepreneurial Opportunities

Season 5, Episode 22 "The Opposite" (4:44)

Season 6, Episode 3 "The Pledge Drive" (3:29)

Chapter 6. Entrepreneurial Product/Service Characteristics

Season 9, Episode 4 "The Blood" (3:58)

Season 3, Episode 5 "The Pen" (2:41)

Season 9, Episode 4 "The Blood" (3:53)

Chapter 7. Entrepreneurial Assessment

Season 8, Episode 1 "The Foundation" (2:43)

Season 9, Episode 9 "The Apology" (4:38)

Chapter 8. Entrepreneurial Adoption

Season 5, Episode 10 "The Cigar Store Indian" and Season 5, Episode 22 "The Opposite" (4:46)

Season 7, Episode 2 "The Postponement" and Season 7, Episode 3 "The

Maestro" (4:14)

Season 8, Episode 9 "The Abstinence" (3:54)

Chapter 9. Entrepreneurial Business Models

Season 8, Episode 8 "The Chicken Roaster" (4:48)

Season 8, Episode 7 "The Checks" (1:52)

Season 7, Episode 20 "The Bottle Deposit" (3:57)

Chapter 10. Entrepreneurial Financing

Season 1, Episode 4 "The Male Unbonding" and Season 6, Episode 5
"The Couch" (3:33)

Season 8, Episode 3 "The Bizarro Jerry" (4:17)

Chapter 11. Entrepreneurial Planning

Season 9, Episode 17 "The Bookstore" (3:02)

Season 8, Episode 21 "The Muffin Tops" (4:22)

Chapter 12. Entrepreneurial Pitching

Season 3, Episode 14 "The Pez Dispenser" and Season 4, Episode 13
"The Pick" (4:26)

Season 9, Episode 16 "The Burning" (4:38)

Chapter 13. Intellectual Property Protection

Season 7, Episode 6 "The Soup Nazi" (4:19)

Season 8, Episode 11 "The Little Jerry" (4:41)

Season 9, Episode 19 "The Maid" (4.29)

Season 7, Episode 7 "The Secret Code" (3:57)

Season 9, Episode 14 "The Strongbox" (2:47)

Season 9, Episode 8 "The Betrayal" (4:21)

Chapter 14. Entrepreneurial Marketing

Season 5, Episode 8 "The Barber" (2:43)

Season 5, Episode 2 "The Puffy Shirt" (4:56)

Season 7, Episode 22 "The Invitations" (3:13)

Chapter 15. Founding Team

Season 9, Episode 18 "The Frogger" (4:46)

Season 9, Episode 14 "The Strongbox" (4:57)

Season 9, Episode 19 "The Maid" (4:48)

Chapter 16. Entrepreneurial Advice Networks

Season 3, Episode 15 "The Suicide" (4:25)

Chapter 17. Social Entrepreneurship

Season 9, Episode 2 "The Voice" (4:46)

Chapter 18. International Entrepreneurship

Season 3, Episode 8 "The Tape" (4:51)

Season 2, Episode 2 "The Pony Remark" (4:42)

Chapter 19. Criminal Entrepreneurship

Season 7, Episode 16 "The Shower Head" (3:55)

Season 8, Episode 4 "The Little Kicks" (4:37)

Please join me for more adventures into the world of entrepreneurship. Until then, have a "liven" good day . . . I know I will!